Subordination

Subordination

Feminism and
Social Theory

Clare Burton

George Allen & Unwin
Sydney London Boston

First published in 1985
George Allen & Unwin Australia Pty Ltd
8 Napier Street, North Sydney, NSW 2060, Australia

George Allen & Unwin (Publishers) Ltd
Park Lane, Hemel Hempstead, Herts HP1 4TE, England

Allen & Unwin Inc.
Fifty Cross Street, Winchester, Mass 01890, USA

National Library of Australia
Cataloguing in Publication entry:
Burton, Clare.
Subordination.

Bibliography.
Includes index.
ISBN 0 86861 718 0.
ISBN 0 86861 710 5 (pbk.).

1. Feminism. 2. Women and socialism. I. Title.

305.4

Library of Congress Catalog Card Number: 84-73433

Typeset in 9/11 Century Schoolbook by Eurasia Press (Offset),
Pte Ltd, Singapore
Printed by Wing King Tong Printing Co. Ltd, Hong Kong

Contents

Acknowledgements

The emergence of the women's movement around fifteen years ago escaped my attention for a while, immersed as I was in domesticity and tiny children. Eventually its existence forced me to ask myself questions about my situation. My early ventures into feminist groups developed into a firm commitment and I have remained actively involved in the women's movement and in women's groups within and outside the trade union movement. The initial concern with my own situation and that of women in general gave place in time to an increasingly specific awareness of the situation of working-class women and their families. I felt the need to develop a conceptual framework which would help to clarify for me the contradictions of a feminist movement within a class-structured society.

My first debt is to the women's movement. I owe much to one particular person I met in the early years of feminist activity, Joyce Stevens, who is perhaps unaware of how important she was, as mentor and friend, in my transformation from a wife and mother into a person.

A number of people have helped me in various ways. Doreen Langley, Principal of Women's College, Sydney University, was a most important influence on me, giving me confidence in my academic pursuits during difficult times. As an undergraduate at Sydney University, I was taught Anthropology by Chandra Jayawardena, who later became my professor in Anthropology and Comparative Sociology at Macquarie University. Chandra is no longer alive, but I share with many others a debt to him. He was an important influence on my development as a teacher and a researcher.

My PhD supervisor, Bob Connell, has already received public acknowledgement for the support he has given to feminist researchers. He took on his role as supervisor of my thesis on the condition that I completed it. Without his insistence that I make that commitment to myself, and without his faith and encouragement, I might not have done. Bob and his associates through their writing have also been a significant feature of the Australian feminist landscape, and my book refers to some of their work.

Dean Ashenden's discussions with me and his scribbles in the margins of an earlier draft of this manuscript are perhaps the most important and lasting contribution to the ways in which my theoretical approach is developing. His insistence on seeking out paradoxes, ambiguities and contradictions in the social world and analyses of it is one that I hope I will always share.

Robin Mackenzie, friend and colleague, read drafts, pondered over my strange sentences, and taught me less than he would hope about the English language. He provided emotional and intellectual support through the entire period of writing.

I owe a great deal to my 'structural substitutes', people who helped me with childcare and domestic labour during critical writing periods. Elizabeth Manson, Sue Taylor and Sally Taylor and their friends, and my former husband, Peter Krinks, all provided me with emotional support, time and care.

The following acknowledgements go back to the years when this manuscript was in draft form for a PhD thesis. It has since been revised again for publication. For their help at various stages in this process I would like to thank Annette Hamilton, Margie Jolly, Gill Bottomley, Brian Fegan, Shirley Dean, Heather Williams, Nick Modjeska, Sue Taylor, Sherry Moriarty, Dave Morrissey, Bob Debus, Tony Branigan, Pieter Degeling, Peter Krinks, John Burton, Cecily Parker, Robert Parker, Ian Bedford, Ann Game, Rosemary Pringle, Kerry James, Pam Benton, Jill Matthews, Sandra Kessler, John Hambley, Caroline Ifeka-Moller, Venetia Nelson and Hester Eisenstein. I am grateful, too, for the comments of anonymous readers of an earlier manuscript. Teresa Brennan, Mia Campioni, Liz Jacka and Liz Gross patiently discussed with me the material I worked on in relation to psychoanalysis.

My children deserve the greatest acknowledgement of all. Rachel, Stephen and Kate are my joy and inspiration.

Technical Note

As I am dealing here with the development of ideas over time, it is particularly important to be precise about the dating of individual contributions to the flow of debate and discussion. Many of the more influential of these sources have been reprinted for wider circulation some time after their first appearance. I have therefore indicated in the text dates of both initial and of subsequent publication, in cases where I am referring to the later source. Initial publication dates appear without brackets. Dates of subsequent publication are bracketed. Both dates are given only on first citation of a work. Thereafter I simply give the date of the publication to which I have myself referred.

In the bibliography this convention is reversed. In cases where there are two dates of publication, the initial date is enclosed within an extra pair of brackets.

The symbols : :: : mean 'is to' 'as' 'is to': hence, male: public: : female: private means 'male is to public as female is to private'.

To Rachel, Stephen and Kate

Introduction

This book is essentially a history of ideas developed in the socialist-feminist tradition during the 1970s. I hope to provide a guide through the maze of a sophisticated and rapidly growing literature. Under capitalism, feminism is an activist and interventionist theory, just as socialist theories of class structure are. Both, together and separately, develop constructs for analysing the social world in order to understand how it can be changed. There has been an added concern, in both cases, to change social theory itself. Feminism is related to a wider body of social theory and it is important to understand its impact on that.

The book reviews central themes in the development of contemporary Marxist-feminist thought: in particular, discussions of the origins of female subordination related to the work of Engels; the use of dichotomies like public/private; the debate over domestic labour; theories drawing on psychoanalysis; and explorations of the relationship between state activities and the subordination of women. Sufficient summary of different theorists' ideas is provided so that the critical analysis may be useful. One of the book's purposes is to draw together strands of thought and debate often kept separate, partly because of disciplinary boundaries, and partly because of how these boundaries have been drawn in different societies as the outcomes of the local terms of intellectual debate.

I have attempted to draw on major theoretical developments in Britain, the United States and Australia with particular reference to the contributions of Australian theorists (see Barrett, 1980 for a British treatment of the same themes). Such a comparative perspective is becoming more important as different countries establish their particular forms of legal redress against discriminatory practices, closely observing each others' progress. Some of the clear differences in theoretical advance between, for instance, the United States and Britain, were developing before the moment when legislative initiatives were going beyond anti-discrimination laws—affirmative action and legal guidelines on comparable worth being examples. These developments have an effect on the way ideas are disseminated; we in Australia, though accustomed to identifying more closely with British theorists than American, are nonetheless taking more notice of the American literature that has an immediate bearing on our own political strategies. This has its effect on our theorising.

The focus of attention is on how, and how far, theorists have been able to point to ways of explaining the 'changing but enduring' nature of sexual inequalities. I am concerned with the ways in which these are reproduced, because unless we understand the basis of their durability in rapidly changing circumstances, effective political interventions to eliminate them will be neither adequately formulated nor acted upon.

I turn now to some preliminary definitions. First, the term 'feminist': it does not, of course, refer to a single category or theoretical position. Indeed, the feminist movement in its early years was deeply concerned with the delineation of its internal political and theoretical differences. Groups with clearly differing goals and principles emerged in the United States, Britain and Australia. Many of these self-consciously labelled themselves as 'liberal feminists', 'radical feminists', and 'socialist feminists'. (For early histories of many of these groups, and how they have differed theoretically, see Hole and Levine, 1971; Mitchell, 1971; Diggs, 1972.)

As I use the term, 'liberal' feminism is concerned with the discrimination against all women in our society. It concentrates on legislative reform and attempts to promote attitudes favourable to women's equality. If this is done without regard to the very different situations in which women are found, the activities implied in this approach may benefit only privileged females inside and outside the paid workforce.

'Radical' feminism, discussed in various parts of this book, holds as its main proposition that the relationship between the sexes is more fundamental and a longer-standing source of oppression than any other. Furthermore, as an organising principle, it constitutes the basis of all human societies, class and pre-class. The political implications of this approach are either utopian (see chapter 3) or they concentrate on all women to the neglect of those men who in a patriarchal order are exploited as wage labourers.

'Socialist' feminism taken as a whole is perhaps the least coherent body of thought. However, it has provided the most important advances in our understanding so far and undoubtedly represents the main direction of future developments. In the early years of the women's movement the term 'socialist' feminism covered ideas compatible with those informing the left wing of the labour movement as well as the views of feminists who rejected the 'male chauvinism' of Marx and the 'male left' in general. The integration of these elements has, with time, become more thorough. Increasingly, 'socialist' feminism as a general body of thought has come to predominate in the literature and is increasingly informed by understanding which derives from the work of 'radical' feminists. Socialist feminists have, of course, drawn extensively on the Marxist tradition, but on many other sources as well. The intersection of Marxist and feminist concerns has been extremely fruitful but it has made clear the need for lines of enquiry more broadly conceived than either tradition has independently allowed in the past. The term 'Marxist' feminism is therefore one of narrower scope than 'socialist' feminism, but in this book the two are often used interchangeably.

In reviewing this body of literature I am also developing an argument of my own on the present and future directions of enquiry into women's subordination in advanced capitalist societies. I argue for a shift in focus from modes of production to processes of legitimation of capitalist social relations. In my view relations between the sexes in different parts of the class structure are not the same. The constructs, 'femininity' and 'masculinity' need, at the least, to be examined in class-specific contexts, rather than in relation to capitalism as a totality. The differences between women of different classes, and within different parts of the working class are more significant than their common gender identity.

I argue in this book that female subordination is not a universal feature of human societies. Where subordination exists, it is the particular variety that must be accounted for. It is in this context of variability that the term 'patriarchy' can be analysed and given more specific meaning. In other words, there can be no general definition of patriarchy. Its manifestation within particular social formations at particular historical moments must form the basis of its meaning.

My understanding of patriarchy gives primacy neither to the family nor to the labour process. Indeed, given the dynamic interrelationship of both, and the contradictions inherent in each, 'patriarchy' cannot be conceptualised in either sphere separately. It cannot be located in one institution (the family) nor in terms of one power relationship or process (control over biological reproduction, or over the social relations of production). The threads of patriarchal relationships lie everywhere in capitalist social formations, as their class-structured nature affects all institutions and social processes.

Some theoretical directions I have found to be less useful than others. I have, for example, excluded a discussion of sex-role theory and its limitations as an explanatory framework for women's subordination (see Burton, 1979). The concept of sex role has had an understandable appeal to feminists. It offers an escape from forms of 'biological determinism' and allows for optimistic programs for overcoming oppression: 'roles' seem relatively accessible to change (Morgan, 1975:135; Benton, personal communication). It is possible, too, that academic feminists had, for a time, little choice about the framework they could adopt. To theorise about sexual inequality in a way that would be acceptable to conventional scholars meant remaining within an orthodox sociological or psychological framework. This is undoubtedly also related to the continuing power of the 'universe of discourse' in which academic women are trained and within which they work.

Nevertheless, to dispense with the sex-role concept seems the only way to demystify what we are talking about and so to shift the theoretical perspective to relationships of control, of domination and subordination. These are the factors ultimately that determine the broad outlines of the behaviour described by role theorists. Only when we have thus shifted the parameters of discussion and analysis can the wider processes which are the pressure points for conformity, acceptance, ambivalence or resistance be located.

My decision was to explore as thoroughly as possible the areas which dominated debate during the seventies. I have thus not attempted to deal with some of the important developments in radical feminist theory. I omit discussion of abortion, rape, men's violence, sexuality, and a range of related issues—for instance, in the discussions of parent-child relationships, there is no mention of lesbian mothers, nor lesbian non-mothers. This is a reflection of the neglect of these issues by Marxist feminism for most of the period under review. It is in these areas that radical feminists have made important contributions, in turn picked up by theorists with a more Marxist focus.

This decision is made easier with the recent publication of an overview of the development of radical feminism in the United States (Eisenstein, 1984) and Matthews' (1984) discussion of heterosexuality as a social construct and the social control of women it affords. Similarly, from a Marxist-feminist perspective, the issues of sexuality and sexual symbolism in the labour process—a significant demonstration of the power of radical feminist ideas within a political economy framework—is developed by Game and Pringle (1983). What this work does is extend traditional Marxist concerns, in ways which I too argue are necessary—to take account of gender as a fundamental organising principle of capitalist economies.

The most significant omission in this book is a discussion of Chodorow's work. In the period I review, Chodorow's writing had little impact on Australian feminists, although this is no longer the case. More attention was given in Australia to British responses to the psychoanalytic debates then current in Europe. Chodorow's work has attracted attention more recently in the context of a developing dialogue between radical and Marxist feminists which has occurred despite the fact that much other radical feminism has developed in a direction not generally regarded as fruitful in terms of political strategy. This means, in retrospect, that it seems important to go back to Chodorow's insights and carefully reconstruct them with closer attention to the gender organisation of the labour process. This would require an extensive analysis of her argument in the context of a broad range of issues, which would be inappropriate in this context. However, some brief comments may be made here about the direction of such an extended rethinking.

Chodorow combines a conception of universal female subordination which derives from 'mothering' with a claim to historical specificity, in relation to industrial capitalism. While I dissent from the postulate of universality, I believe that ideas for political strategy could develop from insights provided by Chodorow, if related more directly to the labour process. If, as she suggests, the sustaining factor for the familial arrangements which perpetuate the effects on people of women's mothering, lies in the organisation of capitalist production and the suitability of these 'masculine' and 'feminine' forms to reproduce it, then the target of change must also lie there. Political intervention needs to be directed to work organisation if men's role in child-rearing is not to become simply a taking over of the sole domain women have been able to claim as their own (see Ehrensaft, 1980). To reorganise family life without this restructuring of work would in any case be impossible. To attempt to do it (through shortening of work hours, flexibility of hours, changes in the organisation of schooling) is to leave intact the fundamental structuring principles of capitalist production and relationships.

To change fundamentally the relations of men with children would have profound effects on capitalism, on the relations between the sexes and on the very construction of gender, and is inconceivable at present, because it would affect all those processes fundamental to capital accumulation. Occupational segregation and the social/sexual division of labour with its accompanying constructions of masculinity and femininity are deeply embedded not only in the process of capital accumulation but also in the legitimation of capitalism as an economic and social form.

I now turn to the structure of the book. Chapters 1 and 2 deal with how commentators on Engels have treated questions about the sexual division of labour in its 'natural' (prehistoric) form as well as in its social (historical) form, and the relation of women's subordination to the processes of human reproduction and to the apparent separation of public and domestic domains. Chapter 3 and those following address the ways in which these questions have been taken further, beyond the confines of

Engels' scheme, and elaborated with particular reference to advanced capitalist societies.

Feminist theory has markedly changed the anthropological enterprise by examining the androcentric bias in much of the ethnographic litera-ture and by introducing new approaches to the analysis of the relation-ship between modes of subsistence and social organisation. Some of this work is examined in the first three chapters.

The tendency to one-directional determinism within some Marxist thought was reflected, for a time, in feminist discussions about domestic labour, evaluated in chapter 4. The 'domestic labour debate' was pursued with the aim of establishing the true class position of all women defined as housewives, but it relied on a class analysis of categories rather than of relationships. It is important to detail this debate, because it lapsed at a vital point, in effect implying the irrelevance of the Marxist theory of value to an understanding of domestic labour (Beechey, 1977, 1978; Smith, 1978). It thereby neglected to analyse the connection between paid and unpaid work in a dynamic way. I examine this relationship in chapter 4 and return to it in chapter 6 where the relationship of domestic labour to state activities is examined.

The study of the reproduction of gender differences has in recent years been pursued in the context of a renewed interest in psychoanalytic theory. In chapter 5 I document the ways in which feminist theorists have re-examined psychoanalytic traditions and literature and the impli-cations they draw for understanding female subordination. Although important, these are insufficient, or restricted, accounts of the reproduc-tion of asymmetrical relationships between the sexes.

The concentration on the state and the education system in chapter 6 is intended to redress this inadequacy. Chapter 6 also looks at policy and feminist theory. Feminists in the three traditions referred to above com-monly make distinctions between policy implications (which emphasise pressure on legislators) and political implications (which are generally referred to an autonomous women's movement). Increasingly, however, the distinction is undermined, particularly as women unionists actively engage in strategies which implicate both. In my conclusions I suggest that legislation designed to eliminate discrimination against women can be used to further socialist-feminist aims.

My concern for legislative reform lies in the belief that it can serve as a vehicle for legitimising many feminist concerns which would not other-wise find institutionalised channels for expression. The legitimation of feminist demands may well come through a use of legislation—in relation to employment, to educational policy, to sexual harassment, to domestic violence—and through demands to iron out the contradictions in current legislation and policy initiatives. Behind every public platform of reform there is a potential hidden agenda which feminists must seize and work with as the basis for more fundamental transformation. After all, many of the legislative reforms are responses to feminist activity. We need to keep our goals and aims clear and not rest until the full implications of each gesture towards our demands are realised and met in further policy initiatives and political action.

Explanation of terms

Feminist or women's movement. I use this term when I am making points about the broad spectrum of feminist activity and ideas.

Women's Liberation Movement. I use this term when I am indicating that the ideas or actions under discussion were not, or are not, shared by liberal feminists working within such organisations as Women's Electoral Lobby in Australia or the National Organisation of Women in the United States. This term also excludes feminist activity within left-wing organisations.

Patriarchy, patriarchal relationships, and the patriarchal-class order. See the introduction for my own understanding of these. See Gough, K. (1973:111) and Komarovsky (1964:226-7) for attempts to analyse the meaning and use of these terms. Gough does this in relation to all societies. Komarovsky makes a distinction between 'masculine privilege' (sanctioned advantage) and 'patriarchal authority' (sanctioned domination) in different segments of the class structure. See also Beechey (1979) for a more recent attempt to come to grips with the meaning of 'patriarchy'.

Mode of production. I use this term only in relation to capitalism. This is because I am not happy with the ways in which other social formations have been categorised into, for instance, the 'lineage mode of production' or the 'primitive communal mode of production'. I would prefer to refer to other types of societies, or social formations.

Social formation. When I refer to social formations, societies and sometimes systems, there is no significance attached to the different words used. The term 'social formation', though, is a useful one: as a theoretical construct it allows for more specific analysis than does the concept 'society' which has different meanings within social theory, in relation to territory, nationhood, government, and so on.

Non-capitalist social formations. I use this to refer comprehensively to all but capitalist social formations, not to a specific type.

Pre-capitalist social formations. Although I am reluctant to use this term, since 'pre-' has an evolutionary ring about it and the term is used to refer to contemporary societies, I use it to distinguish social formations, with which ethnographers have concerned themselves, from the broader category of non-capitalist social formations which would include so-called 'socialist' ones.

'Middle-class'. This denotes higher-status families within the working class.

1

Engels, the search for origins, and feminist theory

> According to the materialist conception, the determining factor in history is, in the last resort, the production and reproduction of immediate life. But this itself is of a two-fold character. On the one hand, the production of the means of subsistence, of food, clothing and shelter and the tools requisite therefore; on the other, the production of human beings themselves, the propagation of the species. (Engels, 1970b:191).

Marxist thought has constantly been important to modern feminism, either because feminist theory has developed within a Marxist framework or because it has been responding to Marxist writings and the practice of political groups espousing Marxist ideas. Within that part of the feminist movement which arose in reaction to the 'male-dominated left', there was a reaction also to the supposed male bias of Marx's writings, and his own work was used to show how little Marxism dealt with the problems of women. For some, the exception was seen to be the work of Engels in *The Origin of the Family, Private Property and the State* 1884 (1970b).[1]

During the early period of the recent feminist movement, anything that Marx or Engels might have said about women, the family, or the sexual division of labour, was pounced upon and quoted by people of different persuasions to prove or disprove a particular point. The fact that this material was scarce simply lent credence to the view that Marxism should be discarded along with the male left, or at least substantially modified. It is only recently that feminists have been concerned to apply the principles of historical materialism to the question of the subordination of women, regardless of questions about the adequacy with which Marx and Engels dealt with it.

In fact both of Engels' long works, written 40 years apart, deal in detail with the family and the position of women. *Origin of the Family* was written in 1884, after Marx's death, but was based on many notes Marx had written on the subject. Engels' book, *The Condition of the Working Class in England* 1845 (1969) was written before Marx and Engels began collaborative work. This work details the changing conditions of working-class men and women with the advent of early industrial capitalism. In addition, the *Manifesto of the Communist Party* 1848 (1969b) analyses prostitution—'public' and 'private', as it is referred to there. The *Grundrisse* 1857–58 (1973), *The German Ideology* 1846 (1969a) and many parts of *Capital* 1887 (1971) also grapple with problems relating to the sexual division of labour and the relation of the family to other aspects of particular social formations. However, among all the works of Marx and Engels it is Engels' book *Origin of the Family* that presents the most comprehensive theory of the development of women's subordination and it has received the most attention as a representative Marxist conception of the origins of sexual oppression.

Origin of the Family did not rely on contemporary empirical data in the way, for instance, that *The Condition of the Working Class in England* did. It was in part based instead on the ethnographic data collected by other people, such as Bachofen 1861 (1967) and Lewis Morgan 1877 (1963), since acknowledged to be inadequate or inaccurate in many important ways; it remains, however, the focus of much discussion. *Origin of the Family* and commentaries on it were central texts to the feminist movement in its early years because of the felt need to understand the origins and subsequent development of the subordination of the female sex. *Origin of the Family* attempted this specifically through tracing its connection to the development of private property and class society.

The following discussion is not concerned with Engels' argument in itself—in its nineteenth-century context and in relation to the historical facts. It is concerned with what mid-twentieth-century feminists *read in* Engels, that is, those themes that were taken up in the body of thought this book is concerned with, and the way they served as a point of departure for theorists looking for the roots of female subordination. I will indicate here the problems which remain central to reformulations of the origins or causes of women's subordination. I refer to work done in the early years of the present phase of the feminist movement. Much of it has formed the basis for further theoretical work, and much of it has since been modified, but a reconstruction of past concerns and interpretations illuminates the contemporary issues.

Problems of historical reconstruction

The most obvious point that Engels makes, simply by trying it himself, is that one can try to reconstruct the past, and find the beginnings of women's subordination.

The 'search for origins' is still an acceptable way of achieving an understanding of women's position and it is a constant theme in the women's issue of *Critique of Anthropology* (1977). In an article entitled 'The search for origins: unravelling the threads of gender hierarchy', Reiter says:

> The search for origins is a theme which unites much of the recent wave of feminist scholarship . . . Before a structure of inequality can be dismantled, we must first know the base on which it rests. Thus our common search for origins is implicitly a search for a strategy with a politicised goal. (1977:5)

Similarly, in the same issue, Aaby writes:

> It is, of course, always problematic to formulate theories about social processes such as the original subordination of women. However, I think it is necessary to try to do so because our ideas of the original character of the relation between the sexes will, consciously or unconsciously, influence the way we conceptualise the process of subordination of women. (1977:49)

We must be perfectly clear about the difficulties in such an endeavour. They are so great, and are there for so many reasons, that my position on this issue is unequivocal: we cannot reconstruct the past in such a way that we will find, in some prehistoric circumstances, the reasons why most women today live under conditions which exclude them from the power resources available to a minority of men.

There has been a great deal of investigation and conjecture about the relationships that held between men and women in prehistoric times. The material ranges from the work of Ardrey (1961, 1966), Tiger (1969), and Morris (1968) on the one hand, to that of Reed (1969), Elaine Morgan (1972), Firestone (1972) and Davis (1972), on the other. A more informed approach has been presented by Kathleen Gough (1972, 1975) who is at neither of these extremes of speculation and attempts to marshall evidence for her contentions from three main sources. On the grounds that 'it is better to speculate with than without evidence' (Gough, 1975:51) she draws on studies of primate behaviour and social organisation, prehistoric archaeology, and ethnographic data from contemporary hunting and gathering societies. Although she recognises the inadequacies of all three kinds of evidence, she believes that, in combination, they may lead to better understanding.

It is necessary to remind ourselves that the results of this sort of reconstruction can only be as sound as the archaeology, primatology and ethnography from which its data derive. Gough herself acknowledges the flimsiness of her sources and the unavoidably speculative character of her interpretations. The most obvious pitfall of writers using these sources of evidence is that they become persuaded of the value and validity of their synthesis; through the force of the combined evidence, they slip into argument from the evidence of the sources taken separately.

For example, after an account of chimpanzee social organisation, Gough says: 'Morgan and Engels were probably right in concluding we came from a state of "original promiscuity" before we were fully human' (1975:59). This is despite her own warning that we should not confuse contemporary chimpanzees with our primate ancestors and despite the contrary evidence she provides from other non-human primates, such as the monogamous gibbon. All primates, she asserts, share characteristics without which the family could not have developed, notably protracted infant dependency which in turn gives rise to a stable mother–child unit. But this says nothing of the other two types of dyadic relationship which would be necessary to constitute the familial form for which she is arguing—that is, relationships between mother and father and between father and child. Male chimpanzees, as she points out, will defend nearby young from danger, but this testifies to some sense of loose community rather than the existence of a family group. To identify the dependency of the chimpanzee infant on its mother with the dependency of human infants on their mothers is to ignore a great deal of empirical evidence and to confuse a known biological link with a supposed social 'fact'. There are widely observed instances in human societies of infants routinely cared for by older siblings or other adults while mothers pursue subsistence activities. (See, for instance, Erikson, 1950; Friedl, 1975; and for European countries, de Mause, 1976; Dunn, 1976.) Moreover, a wide range of primate social organisations exist; the supposedly biologically rooted social–organisational features can simply disappear with ecological variations, and other principles can take their place (Maccoby and Jacklin, 1974; Lancaster, 1976; Crook, 1977).

We do not yet know how much light archaeological evidence can throw on the interpretation of the nature of male–female relationships in the past. The available material can also be misinterpreted. As with the study of contemporary societies, ethnocentric, androcentric and other biases can intrude, for instance, proposing matriarchal theses out of evidence of the existence of female goddesses (Childe, 1963:67). Similarly, Gough's use of the existence of hearths and the use of fire to indicate that there may have been a 'General Headquarters' to which men returned and around which women spent their lives (1975:60) is not a thesis which can be sustained; it is necessarily already based on an assumption of a sexual division of labour and female immobility (the result of women's childbearing and childrearing tasks). Archaeological evidence will perhaps never be enough to provide answers about the position of women in prehistoric times, but it has a great deal more to offer than has usually been acknowledged. Unfortunately, what there is of it has often been harnessed to speculative theories as evidence for already formulated assumptions.

There are similar problems in using contemporary hunting and gathering societies as evidence of our past. As Harris (1968:156) says,

> It is a serious error to suppose that contemporary band-organised hunting and gathering societies are representative of the great bulk of paleolithic hunting and gathering groups. Almost all of the ethnographically classic cases of band-organised hunters and gatherers are marginal or refugee peoples driven into, or confined to, unfavourable environments by surrounding groups of more advanced societies.

Such societies give 'valuable clues', as Gough (1975:52) puts it, but not to the *history* of women's position so much as to the ways in which this position is variable. Leacock (1972:66), who relies on a particular form of evolutionary theory for her attempt at historical reconstruction, acknowledges the oversimplification involved in retrospective evolutionary theory:

> By hindsight, mechanical materialism seems to work. The objective conditions—technological, economic, environmental—that preceded—hence 'caused'—later developments can necessarily and inevitably be located. The more remote the period studied the more the role of internal stresses, alternative choices, and revolutionary versus conservative ideologies that defined precisely how, when, and where major changes were initiated are lost in the ambiguities and spottiness of archaeological and historical data.

This statement recognises the dialectical, contradictory nature of the processes of transformation, of which Engels was so concerned in his theory (if not consistently in his own historical reconstruction).

One cannot dispute that there have been changes in the constitution of some societies from simpler to more complex:

> Archaeological researches have yielded an undeniable picture of mankind's development from 'savage' hunters to 'barbarian' agriculturalists and finally to the 'civilizations' of the Ancient East . . . Meanwhile, ethnographic data have made it increasingly clear that fundamental distinctions among societies at different productive levels underlie the variations among individual cultures. (Leacock, 1972:17)

But here is the crux of the issue. Despite any intention to the contrary, the evolutionary approach to the position of women tends to present a thesis of linear causality—one which can be typified as an economically-determinist position. It relies, through the notion of 'stages', on the development of the productive forces of a society. It cannot consider the organisation of the social relations of production, which does not automatically follow from the nature of the productive forces and about which we do not have the same material evidence. Not only are ideological processes and political arrangements important here, but they play a part in the direction of the development of the productive forces to which is attributed so much importance.

Some of the same problems obviously apply to analyses based upon other people's field work. The use of secondary material is a particularly common practice (and, more recently, a very common practice among Marxist anthropologists and feminists). The work of Meillassoux (1975) is a case in point. His work has been extensively criticised, reworked and reinterpreted. (See, for instance, Terray, 1972; Aaby, 1977; Edholm et al., 1977; Mackintosh, 1977; O'Laughlin, 1977). Other instances of this sort of work have been more solidly based. I will, for example, have occasion to refer to Gough's re-examination of Evans-Pritchard's work on the Nuer (Gough, 1973). This is a careful reappraisal of a kinship system by an anthropologist who is familiar with the intricacies of such systems through field work of her own. However, I also refer to Sacks' work, which uses material from four East and South African societies, drawing on the work of Turnbull (1965), Krige and Krige (1943), Hunter (1936) and Roscoe (1965).[2] Her use of secondary material was very select and in accord with her theoretical orientation. This prevents her from paying sufficient attention to either the ideological or the political mechanisms that mediate contradictions in the relationships between people. I will have occasion to refer to ethnographic material relating to the societies Sacks discusses, and to indicate that more attention needs to be given to the ways in which social formations are reproduced or transformed.

It is interesting to note that those writers who believe that the search for origins is a worthwhile project are not necessarily those who maintain the universality of patriarchy, and vice versa.[3] Mackintosh (1977) assumes that patriarchy has been universal, but rejects a search for its origins. Arguing against Meillassoux's (1975) historical reconstruction, she says, 'we should seek rather to grasp the way in which specific forms of these oppressions operate, how they are maintained and reinforced, how they are overthrown or why they are not overthrown. This is the level at which we should seek to construct theory' (Mackintosh, 1977:121). The more recent writers who posit a universal subordination of women, based on men's control of women's reproductive labour, agree with Mackintosh's view (Bland et al., 1978; McDonough and Harrison, 1978). The opposite position—that women have not always been subordinated to men, but that it is worthwhile trying to trace the origins of the subordination—is an equally respectable position.

Reiter (1977) argues that a search for origins must be carried out, that in fact it is a task all feminists share. While I disagree with her here, her approach allows her to go beyond some of the rudimentary dichotomies that characterise other theories: class/pre-class, state/non-state, and public/private. Her way of reconstructing the past begins with the present.[4] She believes that 'critical junctures' can be identified, in which 'gender relations have changed qualitatively' (1977:6). She discusses the origins and effects of modern capitalism, the origins and processes of 'pristine' state formation and the characteristics of gender organisation in 'original human society' itself. Clearly there are problems here, particularly as the last two steps must rely either on speculative data or on evolutionary assumptions. Reiter does, however, make the important point that state development is not linear:

> A plethora of ranked chiefdoms, proto-states, city-states, feudal domains, empires and even national states have perished over a span of millennia during which the political apparatus we now identify as 'the state' evolved. In over-generalising, we ignore history, and the context in which political formations change. (1977:9)

She also looks at non-human primates and contemporary hunting and gathering societies, not in order to generalise but for evidence of the flexibility of gender roles and their variability in different contexts (1977:14). Though Reiter's approach acknowledges such a variability, it does sometimes assume the existence of cultural constraints that make the allocation of gender roles universal and social organisation along gender lines inevitable. Further, this form of reconstruction may leave us with little to go on in that it may neglect some aspects of the history of an element such as its mythical or oral tradition.

Attempts at reconstruction of the history and evolution of women's subordination relate to the problem of conceptualising the original, 'natural' division of labour, to which I now turn.

One assumption made by Marx and Engels in all their work dealing with the 'primitive communal' society was that the division of labour by sex in this egalitarian system was a 'natural' one. Engels did not say this unthinkingly; he made the point that the causes of the division of labour between the sexes are entirely separate from the causes of the varying statuses that women hold in different societies:

> Division of labour was a pure and simple outgrowth of nature; it existed only between the two sexes,' (Engels, 1970b:317). The division of labour between the sexes is determined by causes entirely different from those that determine the status of women in society. Peoples whose women have to work much harder than we would consider proper often have far more real respect for women than our Europeans have for theirs. (1970b:227)

It is clear that Engels' remarks refer only to the original, 'natural' division. He describes most carefully how conditions which began as 'natural' became oppressive, through changes in the social relations of production. If we needed to interpret him correctly (which, I believe, we do not—our task is to make sense of the social world, rather than disprove Engels' idea of it) we could kindly suggest that he was referring to the division of sexual labour, rather than the social-sexual division of labour, and that he thought no more of it.

However, what remains at issue for us is the very notion of a 'natural' social-sexual division of labour. Engels' views of the 'natural' division of labour are increasingly being replaced by the idea of complementariness as the variability in patriarchy is being recognised, and as a variable sexual division of labour is discovered through cross-cultural research (Mead, 1962; Oakley, 1972). This idea of complementary relationships has to be pursued with caution, for we know within our own society with what force the 'separate' or 'different but equal' ideology is held. To reinterpret other systems with this argument in mind may well be just as incorrect.

There are different ways in which this idea of complementariness is held. Both Aaby (1977) and Reiter (1977) substitute complementary for equal or natural, in the primitive communal society, in order to explain the changes that later occurred. Aaby argues that this equal but different relationship changed with the advent of private property to one of the 'reification of women', which he defines as 'a direct or absolute control of the person itself or some of its activities (reproductive potential, labour power, sexuality). The person or its activities are transformed into an owned object' (Aaby, 1977:36).[5] Reiter argues that as kinship becomes less important as an organising principle and the state more so, there occurs an increasing subordination of women. Engels referred to a similar shift, but it has been feminist writers who argue that women are more firmly incorporated into kinship structures than men. This incorporation is usually located at a structural (or 'unconscious') level (Bland et al., 1978:156) or, more simply, at the empirical level based on data which indicate that women are more closely connected to their kin than men (Mitchell, 1975).[6]

Sacks (1976) modifies an earlier position (see chapter 2) to argue that complementary relationships between the sexes may have existed in non-state societies, and that it is our hierarchical way of thinking, through living in a state society, that introduces a bias in our assessment of other societies. She draws on work carried out in relation to the Iroquois (Brown, 1970; Miller, 1974), the Eskimo (Briggs, 1974) and the Nuer (Gough, 1973; Singer, 1973). There are dangers of romanticising non-state societies in this way, as can be seen in the example Sacks presents of the Eskimo: 'The question "Which is better (or more important), a good hunter or a good seamstress?" is meaningless in Eskimo; both are indispensable' (Sacks, 1976:568, quoting Briggs, 1974). One could say the same about housework under capitalism, but it tells us nothing about the effects of this sexual division of labour in wider economic, political and ideological terms. One would need to look further than the technical, sexual division of labour to see whether equality was maintained throughout the system. That the Eskimo say this, or that one can measure women's productive labour, says little about how women are dealt with in other spheres.

The importance of the distinction between a division of sexual labour and a sexual division of labour is to point to the difficulties in referring to a 'natural' phenomenon—the biological fact of women's reproduction—in social contexts. The difficulties lie in extrapolating from this fact to assumptions of a 'natural' (or complementary) division of social and economic tasks between the sexes.

Prehistoric origins

There are two main versions of the search for 'ultimate origins' of women's subordination, and one can hardly say that either remains faithful to Engels' narrative, since he says, '[t]hat woman was the slave of man at the commencement of society is one of the most absurd notions that have come down to us from the period of Enlightenment of the eighteenth century' (Engels, 1970b:226).

Gough's account is perhaps the clearest in thinking about what an original 'natural' division of labour between the sexes could have meant. The other version to be examined here postulates the primacy of women's oppression in temporal terms, thereby overturning the sequence of events to which Engels devotes most attention—the subordination of women subsequent to the development of private property and the formation of classes. It is important to draw attention to some of the details of these formulations because of their influence on the politics of the contemporary feminist movement.

There is another reason to devote attention to Gough's work. She is an anthropologist who has had a wide feminist readership and is still a constant reference point, as the women's issue of *Critique of Anthropology* (1977) shows. Her extensive research has been carried out over a long time. Her work in the areas of kinship and marriage are the better known among anthropologists: many of us grew up on her contributions to the field of matrilineal kinship in general and her work on the Nayars of South India in particular (1959). This was an important re-examination and modification of the usual definitions of marriage and the family. She has more recently written on the colonial context of the anthropology discipline. In the same way that a 'radical sociology' emerged in the 1960s, Gough contributed to a 'radical', reflexive, anthropology (see Gough, 1968).

Her reception by feminists has, on the whole, been uncritical. This is partly because she bases a lot of her writings on her own field work; her knowledge of matrilineal societies is first-hand and extensive, and her contributions to debates on them remain important (see Schneider and Gough, 1961). She is one of the anthropologists who has moved away from a traditional perspective and has worked on the questions raised by feminist and other political movements. I refer in particular to her article, 'The origins of the family' 1971 (1975), an article frequently cited in sociological and feminist literature.[7]

Gough, believing that women's subordination is connected to the development of family life, seeks to understand its origin through an investigation of the beginnings of the family. She sets out to explain how and why the family originated, what functions it fulfilled in the evolution of humanity and how the original 'natural' division of labour between the sexes later became oppressive.

Gough assumes that in early forms of society and in contemporary hunter-gatherer and horticultural societies, the division of labour is 'natural'. She sees it as being functional and involving neither exploitative nor oppressive relationships: '[I]t was largely a matter of survival rather than of man-made cultural impositions. Hence the impression we receive of dignity, freedom, and mutual respect between men and women in primitive hunting and horticultural societies' (1975:74-5).

However, her ambivalence is shown in another statement she makes:

> From the start, women have been subordinate to men in certain key areas of status, mobility and public leadership. But before the agricultural revolution, and even for several thousands of years thereafter, the inequality was based chiefly on the unalterable fact of long child care combined with the exigencies of primitive technology. (Gough, 1975:74)

Here is the clue to many interpretations of Engels. The ambivalence about the original status of women is partly resolved through the conclusion that within the natural division of labour lay the seeds for women's later subordination. Here also is the clue to the 'complementary but equal' argument. Differences can be thought of as fairly unimportant until a later date—namely, with the division of people into owners and non-owners of the means of production (including labour). Women were implicated in the changed power relationships and this is the theme elaborated by many commentators on Engels' work.

The problems in Gough's account need bringing out since much contemporary writing continues to refer to the family as the main site of women's subordination, arguing for the specificity of patriarchy lying in the relations of reproduction which are in turn found within the family (Bland, McCabe and Mort, 1978).

'The trouble with the origin of the family,' as Gough writes, 'is that no-one really knows' (1975:51), but she proceeds to suggest that it emerged at some time between two million and 100 000 years ago. Further, in her view, it has become universal. 'Some kind of family exists in all known human societies.' The entity she has in mind is '[a] married couple or other group of kinfolk who co-operate economically and in the upbringing of children, and all or most of whom share a common dwelling' (1975:52). But her main concern, rather than being with 'the family', is with particular relationships—especially those relating to the defence and protection of women and children. Gough refers, in relation to pre-state societies as contrasted to primate social organisation, to 'an increased capacity for love, not only of the mother for her child . . . but of

male for female in enduring relationships' (1975:74).[8] She points to the
'generosity and moral orderliness of primitive family life'. She admon-
ishes other feminists—and rightly so—for developing theories which
assume consciously hostile, or power-greedy motives on the part of males
who conspired to 'overthrow' the domination of females.

The universality she attributes to the family is hardly surprising.
Gough defines her unit elastically and thus is able to find it everywhere
through a million or more years of human evolution. All societies have
groups of people who live together, care for children, and cooperate in
economic tasks: *households*, that is, of one sort or another. However, the
variety of possible residential arrangements based on kin or other ties is
great, and households differ widely in such fundamental matters as production, consumption, and cooperation in work and the care of children.
The family, then, cannot be analysed as a discrete entity. 'The family' as a
construct needs to be dissolved. It is not a 'thing'. What really needs to be
examined are relationships—between people, between people and objects,
and between people and ideas—all of which, in this and other accounts,
are clustered around the idea of the 'family'.

On the assumption that it is possible to identity one universally relevant institutional form, Gough confines her attention to the sex-based
division of labour within the family when she is in fact analysing a
social-sexual division of labour within a wider community. If an analysis
is confined to a single institution in this way, all its conclusions are
similarly confined; they are restricted by the initial assumption of the
existence and importance of this institution.

This set of assumptions leads to an oversimplified conception of the
ways in which women's subordination in capitalist societies can be overcome. Gough argues that women have always, in some ways, been subordinate, but that women's position declined further with the advent of
settled communities and the accumulation of property, and began to rise
again with the advent of industrialisation. She explains the growth of the
division of labour in society and within the family in this way: 'With the
growth of class society and of male domination in the ruling class of the
state, women's subordination increased, and eventually reached its
depths in the patriarchal families of the great agrarian states' (1975:75).
She argues that women's subordination is no longer necessary. The factors accounting for this change no longer operate and women's subordination can now be overcome by means already at our disposal. 'The past
of the family does not limit its future ... The sexual division of
labour—until recently, universal—need not, and in my opinion, should
not, survive in industrial society. Prolonged childcare ceases to be a basis

for female subordination when [the means] available allow it to be shared by men.'

In summary, Gough's underlying assumptions are these: originally, the sexual division of labour was 'natural', although it involved some degree of subordination of women. The key to this situation was women's relative immobility, and their lesser physical capacity. With changes in the productive forces, their role involved their confinement to the family while males pursued the important political and economic tasks. However, the technological means have now become available to release them from this confinement, and this should now occur.

Gough does not ask *why* women are subordinate still. Her approach results in a form of moral voluntarism and cannot get a grip on the apparent intractability of women's oppression. Here, as in the general evolutionary model, the productive forces and their development are the determining factors for change: 'The exploitation of women that came with the rise of the state and class society will presumably disappear in post-state, classless society—for which the technological and scientific basis already exists' (1975:75-6).

It is intriguing that Engels' chronology of events has been used, on the one hand, to support a thesis stating the primacy of women's oppression, and on the other to support an argument that hinges upon the connection between class society and women's subordination. Let us look now at the first of these.

It has been assumed that Engels asserts the temporal primacy of women's oppression both by those who would like to refute it and by those who would use him precisely to support that position. I will look at these uses of Engels but I will also point to some errors in interpretation that have been embodied in theory: the time to set the record straight here is long overdue.

Kate Millett, in *Sexual Politics* (1972), deals with Engels in some detail and makes valuable comments on aspects of his work which have been misconstrued by other writers. This is particularly important because Engels' work has been used to elaborate a theory of matriarchy. Millett also criticises his romanticisation of the proletariat marriage and reviews literature on female sexuality to point to the erroneous assumptions Engels makes about it (Millett, 1972:119, 122). On the other hand, her summary of his historical account overturns the chronology of events that he outlined. In commenting on his thesis, she says, 'Far from being the last injustice, sexual dominance became the keystone to the total structure of human injustice' (1972:120). Millett argues that Engels' account provides the most comprehensive analysis of 'patriarchal history and economy' (1972:108) and reformulates his position thus: '[I]t could be demonstrated that patriarchy was accompanied by . . . the ownership of persons, beginning with women and progressing to other forms of slavery . . . Engels' contention that women constituted the first property is probably true' (1972:111-12).

In her account, the explanation for women's subordination is obscure. By contrast, Engels' thesis is clear: the rise of privately owned property entailed its inheritance, and this required some control over the reproductive lives of women. Engels' explanation needs critical examination, but it is at least positing a material cause for such subordination. The other problem with Millett's summary is that it takes no account of Engels' analysis of slavery, which situates it as a variable institution, depending on other economic and social factors; its connection with women's subordination is therefore not a simple one. The 'gradual evolution of patriarchy' is explained here only in terms of a sexual politics which itself needs further explanation.

The coincidence of class and monogamy, of class and female oppression, is detailed in Engels' argument. He connects exploitation and oppression with the advent of private property and the division of labour between producers and non-producers, the latter having control over the labour and products of the former (Engels, 1970b:231). Again, Engels may be criticised for oversimplification, but it is important to note that this was what he said and that he did not posit the original, or earlier, subordination of women.

Simone de Beauvoir, in *The Second Sex* (1972), pays tribute to Engels and tests out a reconciliation of her existentialist philosophical position with Engels' historical materialism (see especially de Beauvoir, 1972:88-91). Her use of Engels, however, is nominal because she is more concerned to present and substantiate her own theoretical position through a wealth of historical and ethnographic data. She accepts Engels' argument connecting the position of women with the institution of private property: 'Woman was dethroned by the advent of private property, and her lot through the centuries has been bound up with private property: her history in large part is bound up with that of the patrimony' (de Beauvoir, 1972:113). She comes to terms with Engels' account by positing a consciousness which exists independently of material factors:

> If the original relation between a man and his fellows was
> exclusively a relationship of friendship, we could not account
> for any type of enslavement . . . If the human consciousness
> had not included the original category of the Other and an

original aspiration to dominate the Other, the invention of
the bronze tool could not have caused the oppression of
women. (1972:88-9)

Shulamith Firestone in *The Dialectic of Sex* (1972), deals with the
prior consciousness that de Beauvoir put forward by suggesting that
Engels' materialist analysis did not go far enough. If the basic division in
society is that between the sexes, then it follows that a conception of
Other needs to be no more basic than that which exists between the
sexes. The materialism of her approach lies in the biological differences
between the sexes. Thus, she rewrites Engels (Firestone, 1972:20, cf.
Engels, 1970a:133).

Juliet Mitchell also puts Engels aside on a tenuous point in order to
proceed with a form of analysis she regards as an extension, or correc-
tion, of his. In *Woman's Estate* (1971:79) she says, 'Engels effectively
reduces the problem of woman to her capacity to work. He therefore gave
her physiological weakness as a primary cause of her oppression.' This
statement shifts the location of women's oppression from the transition
to a property-based division of labour, which was Engels' proposition, to
the biological condition of women.

Those who read Engels' chronology as a description of the primacy of
the subordination of women, go on to assume that women's subordination is determined by their reproductive functions or relative physical
weakness. An interesting contrary view is that of Evelyn Reed, in *Problems of Women's Liberation* (1969). Instead of treating the biological
reproductive capacity of women as the cause of oppression, Reed sees it
as a source of social power. She put forward the influential proposition of
a matriarchy preceding patriarchy, using Engels as her authority. She
used the term not, as she put it, to describe the power of women over
men, but to describe a 'natural superiority' which, being women, they
did not abuse. She insists that this biological–social 'superiority' which
she attributes to women did not involve relations of domination and
subordination.

Like Engels, Reed has a conception of a 'natural' division of labour. In
relation to her concept of matriarchy, she makes use of the ambiguity in
Engels' account to argue that this can be interpreted to mean the original
social leadership of women. In fact, Engels' conception of a 'natural' division of labour does not make this inference except by virtue of women's
position in the matrilocal gens. He refers to the collective ability of the
women to regulate the productive activity of the men (1970b:226).

Reed situates women's position in the context of egalitarian relationships as one of benign leadership. But she exaggerates the position far

beyond that which is presented in Engels' text. The idea that females have inherently more humane, socially desirable attributes has been one thread in the feminist literature since the beginning of the women's movement. (This is also, of course, a standard theme of the patriarchal response).

Implicit in Reed's conception, then, is either dominance of women over men, or some form of cultural separation. This latter perspective is developed further by Dunbar in an article published in Robin Morgan's anthology of feminist writings, *Sisterhood is Powerful* (1970). Dunbar analyses women as a lower caste. She also relies on Engels' account, but interprets it to mean that 'sexism' lies at the root of civilisation as a result of women's reproductive capacity. Women were required to lead a sedentary life. It was females who developed communities. Men were transient and peripheral, moving in and out depending on their hunting activities (Dunbar, 1970:479). As a result of this pattern women developed food production and animal domestication to the point of self-sufficiency. It was then that it became in the interests of men to settle down within the community. Here there is a conception of two separate cultures and two modes of production (hunting and sedentary food production). 'What we find in re-examining history is that women have had a separate historical development from men' (Dunbar, 1970:479). The male intrusion into the community involved a disruption of the female principle which governed cooperative communal living. Males began to dominate it by imposing their set of values on it.

Though the explanation of the change from communal society to patriarchy—'the world historic defeat of the female sex'—is one of the most difficult points in Engels' account, Dunbar's explanation does not solve the problem. She argues that the males' ability to achieve this takeover was based on the prior existence of secret societies which were formed in reaction to female control of the community (1970:480). Once males were able to remain within the community and subsist, they were able to dominate it and 'enslave' women (see Meillassoux, 1975, and Aaby, 1977). Dunbar concludes her analysis by saying that in contemporary capitalist society the family, and the woman in it, now performs functions for the capitalist class. However, this class consists only of males and it is in the interests of males, not those of capital, which Dunbar represents as being served by the institution of the family: 'At this point in history, white working-class men will fight for nothing except those values associated with the masculine ideology, the ideology of the ruling class—family, home, property, country, male supremacy, and white supremacy' (1970:489). While there may be some truth in this statement—and Engels must be criticised for underestimating the force of bourgeois ideology in relation to the working-class family and the males within it—this thesis leads Dunbar to the position that women form a structural group against men (see chapter 4 for an elaboration of this position).

So from Engels we receive the idea that women were disabled as a result of their physical weakness (Gough, Mitchell) or their reproductive role (Gough, Firestone), or as a result of their more 'humane' values (Dunbar, Reed) or men's more aggressive ones (de Beauvoir, Dunbar, Firestone). We also have the interpretation that women's reproductive capacity was initially an asset (Reed) later undermined by the conspiratorial power of men (Reed, Dunbar, Firestone).

2

Engels, class and women

'The world historic defeat of the female sex' is one of the most difficult points in Engels' account. Grappling with it inevitably leads to attempts to improve upon the connection Engels made between women's subordination and the advent of privately held property. It also leads to the question, *why* did the division between owners and non-owners of the means of production (which should not be confused with a division between producers and non-producers—people who work can nevertheless have exclusive ownership of some of the critical resources of society) involve the exclusion of women from the category of owners? Or, more correctly, why did this division involve the appropriation of their labour in such a way that their status became subordinate? What *is* the relationship between the advent of privately held property and asymmetrical relationships between the sexes?

Many feminist writers[1] have addressed the work of Claude Meillassoux, particularly his book *Femmes, Greniers et Capitaux* (1975).[2] Meillassoux's thesis is that control of the means of production is less important as a factor affecting the continuity or transformation of a social formation than control of the means of *re*production, namely, subsistence and women (1972:100). He locates the origins of male control over women at that point in history when horticultural societies began to develop. Because of the intensification of labour required for this mode of subsistence, he argues, the procurement of labour-power assumes greater importance than the extension of land occupied.

Meillassoux has been criticised for his evolutionism, for his ahistorical assumptions and for his disregard of the variability of women's position in societies of precisely the type for which he argues this need for men to control women. He is correctly charged with confusing biological and social reproduction (Edholm, Harris and Young, 1977; O'Laughlin, 1977).

Aaby (1977) deals with the problem of the 'world historic defeat of the female sex' in a way similar to that of Meillassoux. He assesses the work of Leacock, Gough and Sacks as far as they deal with Engels, and, finding all inadequate (1977:32-3), proceeds with his own interpretation.

> [I]t is necessary to assume the existence of a social institution where the irregularities of biological reproduction made the survival of the group critical. This necessitated an expansion of the social group which made imperative the search for more reproducers, i.e., women. As women were the object of this expansion, they could not simultaneously control it. Therefore, men by seizing and protecting women became their reifiers. (1977:49)

More recent versions of the same type of theory assume the universality of male control over 'female reproductive power' (see Bland et al., 1978:159). The question why men rather than women should assume this control is one which Meillassoux, Aaby and others do not convincingly answer. Aaby's contention confuses men and women of one community with the women of another—why should it not be the community which makes decisions about its own needs? Meillassoux points to the greater physical strength of men, implying coercion. But this ahistorical assumption, reminiscent of Firestone's 'power psychology', even if substantiated, would only explain the means by which women were subordinated. It does not explain the need for men to subordinate women.

Formulations connecting women's subordination to a specific time or conjuncture of events in history implicitly raise the question of the criteria used for evidence of subordination. In a Marxist framework, these are usually formulated in terms of non-ownership of the means of production, including other people's labour, combined with the appropriation of surplus labour from the non-owning producers. All this assumes some power, by the non-producers, or the owners, over those producing surplus (or children, in the above accounts). This power can be manifested in political or ideological ways, but clearly has tangible, economic penalties for the people subjected to the power—that is, they perform labour which is surplus to their own subsistence needs. However, the different modes of appropriation, and the different forms that power can assume, complicate this apparently simple situation in many cross-cutting ways, including the different symbolic weights that can be given to different kinds of work.

The example of slavery might clarify this point. In contrast to Millett, who equates men's ownership of women with 'other forms of slavery', Leacock (1972) is concerned with the historical specificity of the institution of slavery. Slavery cannot be assumed always to be the same phenomenon, either in the relationship between slaves and owners or in

the relationship to the means of production. She points out that in societies which took prisoners of war, the status of such prisoners varied: they
could be given the most onerous of tasks, and in places were killed for
ritual sacrifice. However, they could equally be absorbed into the group
with eventual kinship status either through adoption or marriage. To
assume that the labour-power of slaves is the important factor contributing to the class nature of a system may be incorrect. In the Bugandan
case described by Mair (1965) its importance probably lay less in the
appropriation of slave labour and more in the processes by which slaves
were obtained in the first place—that is, the requirement for more land.
As Leacock says, 'Engels made the point that slavery could not become
economically relevant until labour was sufficiently productive to enable
slave-labour to produce enough and beyond the cost of its own maintenance to release a sizeable group for exploitative roles in society'
(1972:52). This diversion into the area of slavery is instructive now that
we are about to consider the ways in which (an invariable) control over
women's labour has been argued in relation to their subordination.

Class and women's subordination

A detailed exposition and critique of Leacock's Introduction to Engels'
Origin of the Family (1972) allows us to correct the oversimplified ways
in which the class-women connection has been constructed. To Leacock,
the family as an economic unit, the dependence of women on men, and
the institution of monogamous marriage, are all related to the private
ownership of the means of production. These are the three important factors in her understanding of women's increased subordination in class
societies. Here she follows Engels closely. Furthermore she points out, as
Engels did, that the abolition of these institutions will not ensure
women's equality—on two grounds. The first is the obvious one that all
these institutions depend on that private ownership. The second is that
the symbols of women's subordination, of women's place, have effectively informed social and political arrangements and gender constructions and would require attention in their own right if women's equality
were to be achieved. Leacock therefore acknowledges the importance of
political activity by an autonomous feminist movement at the same time
that she recognises that women's oppression cuts across other forms of
oppression and exploitation: '[A]ll oppressive relations are interconnected and embedded in our system as a whole, and . . . only united effort
can effect fundamental change' (1972:45).

In dealing with her introduction I am concerned with the two major arguments—namely that there existed a primitive communal mode within which relationships were egalitarian and that it was the introduction of private property and the family as an economic unit, with women's labour becoming privatised within it, that led to female subordination. Her main thesis is that '[t]he subjugation of the female sex was based on the transformation of their socially necessary labour into a private service through the separation of the family from the clan' (1972:41). Her method is to update evolutionary theory as expounded by Lewis Morgan and modified within an apparently historical materialist framework by Engels (as an example of a Marxist approach to history). Leacock dispenses with two arguments which have, for other writers, assumed central importance for understanding women's position. Using evidence from hunter–gatherer societies, she refutes the argument that women's status is related to her functions of bearing and rearing children (1972:40). Second, she argues that a distinction between the public realm of men and the private realm of women makes no sense in 'primitive communal' society where 'the large collective household *was* the community, and within it both sexes worked to produce the goods necessary for livelihood' (1972:33).

What is important about Leacock's argument is that this primitive communal society is broadly conceived to cover all 'pre-class' societies. Consequently, the force of her argument lies in the assertion that through most of history, in most forms of society, women and men held social positions of equal esteem. Leacock extends the idea of a primitive communal mode of production further than Engels did, and further than most writers dealing with the advent of class society. Her argument that such a communal society existed as the common precursor for all contemporary societies is based in part on her own work among the Montagnais Indians, hunters of the Labrador Peninsula. This group has been written about at different times. With the help of archival research as well as her own field research, she was able to show that the more recent commentaries on this society are in fact witness to the effects of the fur trade, and other European influences, on the development of ideas about private ownership of tracts of land and so on. Before this influence, there was no conception of individual ownership of land or of the animals caught on the land (Leacock, 1972:19–20).

What Leacock is able to do, quite importantly in this context, is to show that androcentric or ethnocentric bias on the part of observers has led them to exaggerate the oppression of women in 'communal' societies. Three examples will suffice.

Leacock refers to material on Australian Aboriginal women, and the usually held conception of their low status 'as evidenced by their exclusion from the important ceremonies of the men and from participation in political affairs' (1972:37). She objects, on the grounds that men are in turn kept out of the secret rituals held by the women: 'In daily life, these Australian women emerge as autonomous participants in the affairs of their people, acting with assurance upon their rights and responsibilities.' (1972:38). Similarly, in relation to Eskimo women (who in the ethnographic literature share with Australian Aboriginal women the reputation of being degraded to an extreme), she says, 'Short biographies of Nunivak Island Eskimo women, one of them a shaman . . . likewise indicate considerable freedom of choice and leeway for women to take the initiative in the running of their own lives' (1972:38). She draws on the example used commonly to indicate Eskimo women's low status: the fact that their husbands lend them to visitors as an expression of hospitality is generally taken to be an index of their extreme subordination (1972:31). This interpretation is based on an assumption, drawn from the context of our own society, that women who are obliged to have sexual intercourse with men of their husbands' choosing must be of very low status indeed. Another example she uses is the way in which the isolation of women in menstrual huts is interpreted as a sign of their inferior status, whereas men's huts, from which women are excluded, are viewed by ethnographers as an indication of males' higher status (1972:40).

Correct as Leacock may be to draw attention to the problem of ethnocentric interpretation, she has merely substituted one interpretation for another. In each case the complexity of the ideas (for example, the beliefs about pollution surrounding the menstrual huts) and the political and economic effects of such practices, need to be examined before an interpretation can be substituted for the argument for women's subordination. Hers is a healthy response to the argument that women everywhere have been subordinate, and she indicates the need to examine this concept of subordination more closely in specific social/historical contexts. But Leacock is led to a cruder version of history than Engels outlined. Despite her attempt to produce a transformational, evolutionary view of history, she presents a dichotomous one: the centrality of her pre-class/class dichotomy precludes from the outset any variation in women's position preceding the emergence of commodities for exchange, which in turn inaugurated 'the exploitation of man by man, and the special oppression of women' (1972:33).

Her evolutionary perspective cannot answer many questions. Why did something occur when it did, in the form that it did, and where it did? Leacock's analysis tends to rely heavily on the intrusion of external factors, and in particular the intervention of European colonialism, as the primary cause of women's subordination in different parts of the world. If all but the productive forces are removed from a conception of the economic structure, then the existence of different forms of property—in terms of ownership, control or rights over aspects of the production and distribution processes—cannot be envisaged in any but a fully fledged class society.

Her unitary conception of private property is based on her narrow conception of the economic structure. When she does loosen the concept, it is to disprove the existence of private property, as in her discussions about rights to land in non-class societies. To Leacock, private property can only exist in a society which is divided into producers and non-producers. This leads her to argue that in all societies without such differentiation, females are not subordinate to males. So, in defence of Engels' connection between private property and the subordination of women, she is forced to interpret data in relation to these societies as if they are egalitarian.

The concept of 'private property' is insufficiently examined in this theory. There are different meanings associated with the term 'property' and empirical data indicate the variability in the manifestation of women's subordination and its connection with property ownership. What are not dealt with in this exposition either are the varied ways in which women themselves react against ideologies of female subordination. In Leacock's theory, not to be autonomous becomes equated with dependence and submission; there is no room here for anything in between. Empirical work is questioning the passivity of women when conditions seem to imply their subordination.

Leacock assumes what is in fact problematic, that is, what were the relations between different categories of people in societies which were not dependent on the exchange of surplus, either within their own boundaries or with another community? What have been the variations in relations between producers? What were the relations between those producing surplus in relation to their own needs, as contrasted to those producing less? What were the relations between categories of people who performed different productive functions? What were the ideological and political structures that existed alongside and integral to these variations in the social relations of production? All these are questions which still form the centre of research and discussion.

Lessons from classless societies

Karen Sacks is an anthropologist who has been contributing to both

feminist and anthropological literature since 1970.[3] She is the author of
an article called 'Engels revisited: women, the organisation of production
and private property' (1974, 1975).[4] The importance of this particular
work lies in her attempt to modify Engels' thesis that 'women's status
became solely subordinate and domestic with the development of male
private property, production for exchange, and class society' on the
grounds that there is 'too much data showing that women are not the
complete equals of men in most non-class societies lacking private property' (Sacks, 1974:213). Sacks argues for variability in women's subordination in pre-class societies and attempts to loosen the connection
between class and female subordination. I argue here that her particular
way of conceptualising this variability is misconceived. But it is important to understand her approach, which is based on a public/domestic
distinction as an explanatory device, because, as we shall see in the
following chapter, this has had an appeal far wider than this particular
debate in anthropology.

Sacks sets out to examine Engels' analysis of the material bases of
women's status as well as his evolutionary framework (1974:213). Her
main argument is that Engels was incorrect to see women's 'wifely ward'
status as an indication of her more general 'social status' on the grounds
that the two have some independent existence (Sacks, 1974:218). She
recognises that they also feed into each other, but it is this relative independence that forms the basis of her analysis.

Sacks' thesis rests on the assumed existence of a concrete (not analytic) distinction between a public and a domestic domain. It is necessary to
determine whether this separation exists, under what conditions and in
what form. Her first proposition is that 'there are two aspects of women's
position—women as social adults, and women as wives—and that these
can vary somewhat independently' (1974:218). There are immediate
problems with the term 'social adult'. This is a difficult concept, considering the variability of 'emic' definitions (used by the social actors as
distinct from the 'etic' categories of the observer) of adulthood.[5] One
could argue that in many systems there is no such idea—rather, there are
'male adults' and 'female adults'. The concept of 'adult' presupposes similarity, identification or equivalence, as against some other category, such
as that of 'child'.

For Sacks, the concept of 'social adult' is related to the idea of a public
sphere. More specifically, the second proposition of her main thesis is
that as far as women are concerned, they are designated social adults
'where they work collectively as part of a productive group larger than or
separate from their domestic establishment' (1974:218). She shares with
Gough and Leacock the assumption that

> in societies based on production for use[,] the performance of
> social labour gives a person the right to join with other
> adults in making political decisions and settling disputes.
> This is because political decision-making and dispute settle-
> ment are responsibilities of adult members of an egalitarian
> society. (Sacks, 1974:216)

Apart from the circularity of this argument, it ignores many variables
which, if they are accounted for at all, are regarded as 'unfortunate' or
'accidental' (such as the fact that the 'domestic business' of wives involves
their exclusion from social–political activities, but that they are nevertheless equally 'social adults' (Sacks, 1974:215)). This does not account
for ideological mechanisms which in some societies maintain the subordination of women; neither does it allow for the fact that in societies where
all adults are producers, some may nevertheless be producing a surplus
for the benefit of others. This may or may not involve the subordination
of the former groups by the latter, a problem to which we will be returning. But it is important to note that it may.

The other problem with the way in which Sacks defines women as
social adults is the confusion between the technical organisation of the
labour process and the social relations of production. Extra-domestic
work groupings are viewed here as an indication of women's higher
status. By confusing 'social production' (as it is understood within capitalism) with collective work, she gives the size or constitution of the
work groups a determining position. Collective work, in its variable
forms, must be understood as one aspect of the total process of
production.

To say that women are social adults when they work collectively is
meaningless unless information is available about the control of the
products of their labour, its distribution, and the entitlement to any surplus that might be produced. The constitution of the work group is frequently important in answering these questions, particularly where kinship relations order such groupings. But that is different from placing
stress on an 'extra-domestic' grouping as something which works against
the subordination of women. One suspects Sacks had the isolation of the
modern housewife in mind and that she was alluding to Engels' emphasis
on women entering social production under capitalism, and to the accompanying assumption of its being a prerequisite for their equality. This is
a theme she returns to in her final section.

In reference to some patrilineal systems, it is somewhat irrelevant
how large or how constituted the women's work group is if the factors of

agnatic descent, exogamy and virilocal residence are operating. One must distinguish de jure and de facto rights in this context and not refer to 'unfortunate' consequences, as Sacks does. This disjunction is common, with the de jure rights being usurped in practice. O'Laughlin (1974) makes this clear in her discussion of the Mbum Kpau, where she says that relatively few politico-juridical superstructures exclude women or relegate them to inferior positions:

> Within a lineage, members cooperate in terms of an ideology of generalized reciprocity ... Theoretically women remain members of the lineages of their fathers even after marriage, thus maintaining their rights to cooperative and craft labour, but with a rule of virilocal residence they are seldom in a position to claim these rights. (O'Laughlin, 1974:308)

So egalitarian rules of property assignment and claims to the labour of others do not, then, reflect the real relations of production which, in the case of the Mbum Kpau, are marked by considerable sexual and age asymmetry (O'Laughlin, 1974:307). Here O'Laughlin argues that consideration has to be given both to the authority of the male elders as well as to the rules of exogamy and virilocal residence, and to people's access to the labour of others in the creation of surplus. This is important in the accumulation of other resources, such as prestige, bride-wealth and, thus, women for the patrilineage.

There is another basis for the subordination of women implicit, but not developed, in Sacks' account. This is related to the situation where women bear children for groups other than their own. This may or may not be a source of their inferiority. Sacks represents biological reproduction as a private, that is, domestic, concern (1974:215). This is to simplify a complex process involving at the least two separate sets of relationships: that between the biological and the social father and the mother, and that between those who may control women's sexual activity and the women themselves, if there is such a division.

Gough, in a re-examination of Nuer ethnography, suggests using a distinction first made by Bohannan (1949), in that 'by separating the rights in a woman as sexual partner and domestic worker from the rights in her as genetrix, affords a certain personal autonomy to women, while retaining at least in theory, the legal principle of agnatic descent' (Gough, 1973:111). She goes so far as to distinguish this situation from the type she would refer to as 'patriarchal':

> In general ... systems which permit the separation of rights *in uxorem* and *in genetricem* are radically different from

various patrilineal kinship systems which are also what we may call patriarchal, in which a woman is legally subordinate to one man, or to one at a time, who controls at once the sexual, procreative and domestic rights in her.

It is necessary to distinguish sexual freedom from the allocation of the results of sexual activity—that is, children—to particular groups. Sacks's material implicitly points to the (public) contradiction between female and male ideology in relation to women's sexual activity. In one of the societies (Pondo) women of the same household (related to each other through the patrilineage of their husbands), cooperate in arranging extramarital sexual affairs for each other, despite the fact that men hold a very firm view about the impropriety of such activity (Sacks, 1974:218). However, the women's children belong to the husbands' groups. A husband may claim compensation for his wife's adultery, but this is purely a matter between men. Sacks, by separating 'private' reproduction from women's sexual freedom, argues the case for women's equality within the public sphere, and inequality within the domestic sphere.

It seems useful to conceptualise the Pondo situation described by Sacks in terms of unequally competing ideologies. There is the important issue of women actively participating in the cultural definition of themselves. This can easily be overlooked. It should not be assumed that all participants are operating consensually in the structuring of relationships, or that women are passive recipients of a male-defined and dominated cultural order. Women are more or less active in this respect (as are men). Any theory of women's subordination is inadequate if it does not take this into account.[6]

It is clear that, for the Pondo, despite the lack of control men have over women's sexual activities, control over the allocation of children is maintained. Compensation for adultery is arranged and the offspring remain within the husband's patrilineage. It is clear that the two ideologies are not competing equally. It would be important, for a fuller understanding, to know more about the processes by which the dominance of the male ideology is maintained, possibly along the lines indicated by O'Laughlin. The women's ideology is not concerned with *allocation* of the children, (crucial as that might seem if one considers why men should control the 'body products' of women at all). The women retire, as it were, while the males negotiate and, by so doing, reinforce their ideology: the right of the patrilineage to the women's children. That a subordinate ideology exists is clear at the level of behaviour, where women are in rebellion but do not, ultimately, challenge the patrilineal ideology.

The third proposition in Sacks' argument is that

> [t]he meaning and status of 'wife' . . . depend on the nature of
> the family in much the way Engels suggests. Where the
> estate is familial, and the wife works for it but does not share
> in its ownership, she is in much the same relationship to her
> husband and his kin as is a worker to his boss. Where there
> are no private estates, or perhaps, where the family estate is
> jointly owned, the *domestic* relationship is a more egalitar-
> ian one. (1974:219)

This is the most difficult proposition to discuss because, in a sense, it has
little meaning in relation to her material. For instance, the 'marital
estate' means little in the context of patrilineage or other control or
ownership of resources. The way in which the problem is formulated pre-
empts alternative interpretations. Consider the Lovedu, for instance.
The Lovedu economy is based on production for use, which for Sacks
means production to meet subsistence needs. She refers to this society as
'egalitarian' though in important ways it clearly is not. It is in this case
that the separation of the domestic and public spheres is crucial to her
theory, since through it Sacks can maintain that women are equal to men
in the public sphere although there is slight discrimination against them
in the domestic sphere (1974:215). The public sphere assumes
importance as the primary domain for establishing equality.

An important source of confusion lies in Sacks's explanation of the
constitution of the domestic domain. She says that major productive
resources are owned by the 'family' whereas, in fact, ownership is vested
in patrilineages, or 'houses' within patrilineages, but not families (Krige,
1974). It is meaningless to refer to 'marital estates' and correlate this
with 'domestic relationships' in the face of a web of relationships
between individuals (male and female) and different 'houses' within
patrilineages, as well as different forms of control and ownership, some
acted upon and some latent.

Within the societies Sacks selected, she defines the Buganda (or the
Ganda, in her account) as a class society. In her analysis of this system
Sacks clearly has her eye not only on Engels' statement about women's
role in social production but also on the solution she presents for women
under capitalism. Sacks stresses these aspects of the Buganda society:
that there were slaves, and in her account it is assumed that their labour-
power was an important factor contributing to the class nature of the
system; that productive resources were individually owned (rather than
being owned by lineages or families); that women worked alone, that is,

they did not participate in collective work groups; and finally, that women produced most of the food (Sacks, 1974:214).[7] Sacks is concerned here to draw a parallel with the position of women under capitalism. I would rather concentrate on the differences, which would appear to me fundamental.

Two points are important. The first is that the subordination of women must be seen in the context of other relations of domination and subordination. It cannot be assumed, for instance, that the advent of slavery is a critical factor per se. In this case slaves were easily absorbed into households and were not important as labour-power: the capturing of land was as important as the capturing of people. It means that the men to whom women were attached have to be analysed too, in their particular relationships of domination and subordination, particularly in relation to the chiefs for whom they worked. Second, it is necessary to stress the contradictions that emerge at the ideological level, as a potential area of transformation. Sacks argues, in relation to the Buganda, that as a domestic domain is increasingly separated from a public one, and as women are increasingly excluded from the latter, women's subordination also increases. She draws a parallel with the domestic sphere under capitalism and women's status in it. She concludes her analysis by drawing a comparison between the Buganda system and capitalism. She refers to the women's work as 'individual domestic production for household use' (1974:214).

Sacks's final comment stresses once again the importance of women as 'social adults'—until they are so regarded, they will remain subordinate. To be so regarded requires them to be involved in social production:'what is now private family work must become public work for women to become full social adults' (1974:222).

To summarise the problems in her argument: the use of a public/domestic dichotomy as an explanatory device leads to the assertion that, once the distinction is dissolved, women's equality will be assured. The distinction itself needs to be specified, as to whether it exists structurally, 'on the ground' or as part of people's ideology. This problem is addressed in the following chapter. The other criticism to make is that her analysis of these systems is based on the assumption that women's subordination under capitalism is based on their confinement to a domestic sphere. But she has contributed to an understanding of the inadequacies of Engels' account, through her attempt to disentangle unitary notions such as 'private property', 'class' and 'subordination'. Her comparative approach has opened the way to a more informed appraisal of Engels' main thesis.

Her work shows the need to deal with the problem of women's sub-ordination at an empirical rather than only at a theoretical level. But it also shows the difficulties involved in using the data collected by other people—difficulties to which I have already referred.

There is a further problem. Ethnographic material is looked at with women under capitalism centrally in mind. Sacks's first paper was based on the assumption that the egalitarianism found among the Mbuti and the Iroquois would give us clues to what were the necessary changes for our own society (Sacks, 1970:455). Similarly, in the article being appraised here, her final section is an analysis of what these four socie-ties tell us about women's subordination under capitalism and what changes must come about. I would suggest that what we learn from other systems is more about the *complexities* of the situation under capital-ism: much anthropological work is simplifying, for instance, the class-women connection. We learn, on the contrary, the many diverse ways in which women's subordination, where it exists, may be perpetuated.

Conclusions

In chapters 1 and 2 I have not attempted to review all of the possibly rele-vant anthropological literature. I have simply outlined some significant feminist treatments of the question. These touch on only a small fraction of the quite heterogeneous range of pre-capitalist societies, so that the result is in no sense a general or exhaustive examination of all the evidence and issues relating to gender construction and social reproduction in such systems. The very extensive category of peasant societies, for example, is left entirely unexamined. Nevertheless, the material, partial, fragmentary and tentative as it may be, has an impor-tant bearing on central themes of this book.

Discussion of Meillassoux's work has been valuable in two ways: it has focused attention on the issue of social reproduction and it has reopened the issue of the 'search for origins'. This search is clearly more defensible when informed by some theoretical conception of what is being sought. If, for example, the connection of female subordination with class is conceived as 'invariant', it is obviously appropriate, as in the case of Leacock's work, to focus on the moment at which classes emerged. There are, however, still difficulties. The assumption of unicausality takes little account of the possible variability of political and ideological factors. Sec-ond, this line of argument tends to involve, implicitly or explicitly, the assumed necessity for men to control the reproductive lives of women.

There is a great deal of evidence that males, or male elders, do not control women's reproductive lives (cf. McDonough and Harrison, 1978; Bland et al., 1978; Eisenstein, 1979). Women have shown their relative independence here in many different systems. We have noted, also, the need to distinguish different types of control over women, even in relation to their reproductive capacity. There are differences between controlling their sexual activity, whether they give birth, whether their children live, and to which groups their children are allocated. In the latter case there is frequently room for negotiation, for variation from the societal norm. But even if there were not, these processes need to be placed in the wider context of mechanisms of social reproduction in all their complexity (see chapter 6). To have details of the former does not provide a sufficient picture of how women's subordination, where it exists, is perpetuated. It has not been convincingly demonstrated that men's control over biological reproduction, or the allocation of children to groups, is indispensable for the reproduction of society in the general sense. Indeed, there seem increasingly solid grounds for rejecting this view. While women's biological reproduction and its control is confused with broader processes of social reproduction, it is too easy to locate the basis of the latter within a sex-gender paradigm.

What we can do now is release the male-female relationship from a determinate position in relation to social reproduction. Engels' understanding of 'private property' with its specific meaning of a division of owners and non-owners of strategic resources needs to be interpreted at a more general level than that of male-female relationships. The particular organisation of the social relations of production, whether they include the existence of slaves, whether one's status is temporary or permanent, all the variations referred to in this chapter, would indicate that women as a category may be disadvantaged or they may not. Other categories of people have been subordinate in the relationship to property ownership and it does not necessarily follow that women have universally been subordinate as a category as well.

The basis for subordination remains as Engels indicated—the existence of categories of people in different relationships to 'private property'. We arrive now at the particular case of capitalist societies—where there is a division of producers and non-producers, and where the property relationship is misrepresented as a relation between people and things, so that production is seen as the fruit of 'property' (for example, capital or land) and not of labour (Bloch, 1975:222). The question now becomes, is there something inherent in the representation of the property relations of capitalist systems which makes the subordination of women inevitable? The following chapters argue that this is the case. A task for the analyst arguing in this manner is to discover the mechanisms through which the subordination of women is perpetuated. Women's subordination, and its different expression in different classes, cannot be understood if the analysis is confined to economic processes. The recent shift of attention from production to social *re*production is therefore critical. The ideological realm is the locus of some of the most important of the mechanisms by which the social relations, including gender relations, of non-capitalist and capitalist social formations are reproduced and changed. Part of our task is to investigate the cultural and symbolic systems by which women's subordinate position appears somehow 'natural'. The ideology of public and private domains, and their association with males and females respectively, is a component of a symbolic repertoire which works, or is active, in this way. An examination of this ideology is the theme of my next chapter.

3

Public and private worlds

> [O]ne important aspect of the conception of the family unit
> which . . . has so far remained fundamental to our social
> structure—the notion that though the members of a family
> must in all their dealings with the outside world acknowl-
> edge individually the impact of the general law, yet among
> themselves they can claim a kind of sacred protection behind
> the door of the family home which, generally speaking, the
> civil authority must not penetrate. It is obvious that in 1957
> the claim is subject to substantial qualifications. For the
> present age is notoriously an age . . of 'meddling'. (Foreword
> to Graveson and Crane, *A Century of Family Law*, by the
> Right Honourable Lord Evershed, 1975:xv)

This quotation expresses a theme which has been echoed in feminist cri-
tiques of conventional views of the family. The following chapters deal
with the many dimensions of a problem encapsulated in the phrase 'the
personal is political'. This phrase is an expression of postulates about
power elaborated particularly by Kate Millett in *Sexual Politics* (1972):
that the realm of the political cannot be divorced from the realm of relationships within the family—or from relationships between people of different sexes, classes and races.

The dichotomy of public and private is an extraordinarily pervasive
idea. This can be seen merely by listing the familiar formulae in which it
has been expressed: public/private, work/home, outer/inner, culture/
nature, impersonal/personal, and so on. These are not simply different expressions of the same thing. Rather, the different ways in which
these divisions are perceived must be placed in social and historical perspective. Even within a particular society the meanings undergo transformation over time, or in different social contexts.

What, then, is the status of the terms, public and private, in relation
to males and females, in societies where there are symbolic expressions of
these categories of thought? Is it enough to argue that these are ideol-

ogical constructs only, and as such they serve to obscure economic and other realities? Can they be regarded as real, thereby expressing the confinement of women to a domestic domain, or at least their exclusion from the public? Or can we presume that they are the privileged knowledge of the theorist, who, through analysis, discovers them at a structural level, of which social actors may not be aware?

This chapter examines particular ways in which a public/domestic separation has been used as a general device for explaining women's subordination. By examining this type of conceptualisation I will show that such divisions cannot properly be used to illuminate the problem. A common proposition is that women's subordination is based on their confinement to a domestic sphere, regardless of whether they are involved in production outside that sphere. This is related in a variety of ways to women's childcare responsibilities or to their role in biological reproduction, or both.

Four main perspectives will be appraised in this chapter: the radical feminist position; a less easily categorised position taken by feminist anthropologists which explores the symbolic expression, across cultures, of separate spheres and their possible origins; a Marxist account which will be enlarged upon in chapter 4; and lastly, the work of sociologists whose focus has been on the ways in which husbands and fathers as wage labourers experience their world. The last group of writers, I believe, provide links in what remains a disconnected argument within feminist thought.

Radical feminism

Radical feminism recognises the oppression of women as a fundamental political oppression wherein women are categorised as an inferior class based upon their sex. It is the aim of radical feminism to organise politically to destroy this sex class system. As radical feminists we recognise that we are engaged in a power struggle with men, and that the agent of our oppression is man in so far as he identifies with and carries out the supremacy privileges of the male role. For while we realise that the liberation of women will ultimately mean the liberation of men from the destructive role as oppressor, we have no illusion that men will welcome this liberation without a struggle ... Radical feminism is political because it recognises that a group of individuals (men) have set up institutions throughout society to maintain this power, (*New York Feminist Manifesto*, cited in Mitchell, 1971:51)

Shulamith Firestone's *The Dialectic of Sex* (1972) is generally regarded as the most thoroughly worked out statement of radical feminist theory and the basic text for radical feminist ideas. Although she differs from some others in her use of what she calls a historical materialist approach, she is not significantly different in the ways in which she fills in the details.

Radical feminism argues that the sex division, or antagonism, is more fundamental than any other, historically and structurally. Firestone's argument is that the biological differences between men and women—or, more specifically, the way in which women, through their reproductive capacity, are tied to their biology—creates a 'sexual class system'. She argues that there is an inequality, in terms of dealing with the world, that is *natural*. The material basis for this inequality is the biological family which requires that women are dependent on men, and children on adults, for their survival. This pattern of dependence has given rise to a 'psychological pattern of dominance-submission' (Firestone, 1972:45) which shapes not only our most intimate personal relations but all institutions in the wider society as well.

Thus she concludes that the power of males is the basis for all forms of exploitation and oppression. Although she argues for the universality of this scheme, she suggests that the modern nuclear family under present-day capitalism 'intensifies the psychological penalties of the biological family' (1972:18). She stresses the connection between women's and children's oppression and, using Ariès' study 1960 (1973) of the development of the idea of childhood, traces the development of the accompanying emphasis on motherhood (Firestone, 1972:76-89).

Firestone relates the process of the privatisation of the family to technological advances, which undermined the economic and social factors ensuring male supremacy, and made additional mechanisms necessary to preserve it. As women's economic independence became possible, there developed ideologies in relation to love, sexuality and childhood, as well as motherhood, designed to keep women (or at least most women) unaware of their subordinate status. The isolation of each nuclear family and these accompanying ideologies made it difficult for women to see that their position was determined socially rather than individually or psychologically. Inequalities were perpetuated by males, to the benefit of males.

In this scheme, Firestone counterposes 'natural' to 'human'. By 'natural' she means inherently unequal, and by 'human' the technological capacity to overcome this: 'Women, biologically distinguished from men, are culturally distinguished from "human". Nature produced the fundamental inequality . . . which was later consolidated, institutionalised, in the interests of men' (Firestone, 1972:192).

In Firestone's view, culture/nature, human/natural, are universal dichotomies; they can only be transcended to the extent that culture can overturn 'nature' and harness it to 'human' (i.e., newly defined) needs. This will only occur, in Firestone's view, by women seizing control of the means of *reproduction* (1972:19). It will then cease to be the basis of women's inequality and—deriving from children's tie with the mother—the oppression of children.

For Firestone, then, the 'private' sphere *is* the family—or more specifically, the women and children within families. In contrast is the 'human' and 'cultural' public sphere of men. It is in this public arena, from which women and children are excluded, that men control ideological production as well as the economic and technological resources of society. Men are in control of the construction of social reality and devise the ways of maintaining it.

An argument which universalises sexual antagonism cannot adequately explain it without recourse to speculation about its origins. Although Firestone's focus is contemporary capitalist society and its technological potential to change, she has difficulty in incorporating into her analysis the full impact of the class structure on the relations between females and males. The structure of class relations is not directly comparable to relations between the sexes as she seems to imply. The influence of class on the changing ideology of patriarchy is not accounted for in this argument. It remains couched in terms of the power of all men as against the powerlessness of all women (and children). Firestone accepts the dominant role that patriarchy plays but fails to analyse the ways in which it intersects with the class structure.

There are two extensions of this type of theory which are not restricted to the radical-feminist approach. The first is that a particular psychic structure for females is claimed to exist as a result of relationships within the family. The second is that the different experiences of men and women, as a result of sex-role allocation, and the exclusion of women from the cultural sphere, leads to the brutalisation of the cultural sphere: it is deprived of some of the emotional resources that women and children could offer. Germaine Greer, in *The Female Eunuch* (1971) agrees with this second proposition: that women can counter violence with love. Both extensions were propounded in classical suffragette theory: that women possess 'domestic' qualities which will humanise the 'public' arena. This is also a widely held notion on the part of many present supporters of the existing order, and can lead to an elevation of the female principle, as women will necessarily be the guardians of human-ity. There are logical difficulties in these arguments, especially if they are based on the proposition that these qualities derive from the social conditions in which they have developed. In Firestone's argument they result from 'natural' conditions.

This is where Firestone's solution is the most radical of all those being examined here. In her view, the 'natural' inequality can only be overcome when there is a complete separation of reproduction from women's lives, so that women and men are made equal through technological innova-tion—the development of artificial reproduction outside women's bodies must take place (1972:206). This requires women's power: should men maintain their control, such a process would not occur. This is a strong argument for a completely autonomous women's political movement and the coming together of all women since in this view, they have common interests which override those of class or race.

The radical feminist perspective, illustrated by Firestone's work, has usefully shown how systematically patriarchal institutions and ideas affect all women (and men, and children). The analysis of love, the role that romantic love plays, the situating of sexuality in historical contexts and their definition as oppressive to women are important points stem-ming from radical feminist arguments. The role that Freud's psycho-analytic theories have played in perpetuating a definition of women as inferior to men, to which Firestone draws attention, will be discussed in chapter 5.

But to claim that patriarchy ultimately determines the position of all women, and dominant-subordinate relationships generally, is not a cred-ible way of understanding the historicity of relations between the sexes—shown especially by the differences between women of different classes or historical periods. The *apparent* division of the world into public and private domains is not merely a prop for male domination; it is also important to the continuing structuring of societies along class lines.

Feminist-informed ethnography

The developing interest in the private sphere, the family, under capital-ism, sparked a response among anthropologists to pursue the importance of this sphere in non-capitalist modes of production. Just as analyses were moving to a recognition of the complexity of the situation within the capitalist mode of production (see chapter 4) a contrary trend towards grand generalisation took precedence in the work of anthropol-ogists, particularly within feminist anthropology. The best example of this line of thought is a book of anthropological readings which uses the public/domestic dichotomy as its central theme.[1] This book, *Woman, Culture and Society*, edited by Rosaldo and Lamphere (1974) includes an article by Ortner 'Is female to male as nature is to culture?' which will be taken as the main text for the following discussion.

The basic argument in the book is that there exist, universally, certain symbolic expressions of the devaluation of females. An appraisal of this approach is made difficult by the fact that the separate male/female spheres have been pursued cross-culturally and through different historical periods as if the various manifestations have some equivalent status or meaning. The separation is variously conceptualised as public/private; public/domestic; culture/nature, and others, to which I later refer. This approach, implicitly or explicitly, draws heavily on Simone de Beauvoir's work, which in its turn combines an existential position with Lévi-Strauss's structuralist approach to male–female relationships and his conception of the nature/culture boundary. De Beauvoir says,

> man never thinks of himself without thinking of the Other;
> he views the world under the sign of duality, which is not in
> the first place sexual in character. But being different from
> man, who sets himself up as the same, it is naturally to the
> category of the Other that woman is consigned; the Other
> includes woman. (1972:100–1).

She goes on to say that women held power beyond the human realm as Earth, Goddess and Mother, and that they are therefore culturally defined as outside that realm (1972:102).

Rosaldo explains what is meant by the public and domestic domains and the theoretical significance they are given:

> In what follows, it will be seen that an opposition between
> 'domestic' and 'public' provides the basis of a structural
> framework necessary to identify and explore the place of
> male and female in psychological, cultural, social and econ-
> omic aspects of human life. 'Domestic', as used here, refers
> to those minimal institutions and modes of activity that are
> organised immediately around one or more mothers and
> their children; 'public' refers to activities, institutions, and
> forms of association that link, rank, organise, or subsume
> particular mother–child groups. Though this opposition will
> be more or less salient in different social and ideological sys-
> tems, *it does provide a universal framework for concep-
> tualising the activities of the sexes* [my emphasis]. The
> opposition does not *determine* cultural stereotypes or asym-

metries in the evaluation of the sexes, but rather underlies
them, to support a very general (and, for women, often
demeaning) identification with domestic life and men with
public life. These identifications, themselves neither necessary nor desirable, can all be tied to the role of women in
child rearing; by examining their multiple ramifications, one
can begin to understand the nature of female subordination
and the ways in which it can be overcome. (Rosaldo, 1974:23)

Ortner's chapter in this book poses the dichotomy in terms of the
nature/culture opposition. She draws on both Lévi-Strauss and de Beauvoir, modifying their position to argue that women are universally conceptualised as being closer to, rather than identified with, nature.

The assumptions underlying this particular conceptualisation of
Ortner's are not intrinsic to all public/private distinctions. A distinction
between public and private in social relations can be argued without
resorting to biological differences. In Ortner's theory the two types of
argument are connected, a common approach by anthropologists who
attempt to use cross-cultural symbolic expression to understand better
the nature of the family within the capitalist mode of production. The
symbolic distinction of culture/nature is equated with the public/private
distinction which has been postulated as a basis for understanding
women's position within capitalist society. Ortner argues that women are
identified with, or seem to be a symbol of 'something that every culture
devalues, something that every culture defines as being of a lower order
of existence than itself. Now it seems that there is only one thing that
would fit that description, and that is 'nature' in the most generalised
sense' (1974:72). She disputes that women are identified with nature as
against culture, because women are clearly active agents in a social context. Indeed, part of the sexual division of labour usually involves women
in transforming natural objects into cultural objects—in particular,
through socialising children and cooking food. Ortner argues that our
understanding of women's devaluation must, at the very least, take into
account her ambiguous position in this regard.

Her thesis, then, is that despite the objective equal status of women
and men as human beings, women are symbolised as closer to nature as a
result of three aspects of their lives, all based on their procreative role:

> (1) woman's *body and its functions* [are] more involved
> more of the time with 'species life'. . . (2) woman's body and
> its functions place her in *social roles* that in turn are con-
> sidered to be at a lower order of the cultural processes than
> man's; and (3) woman's traditional social roles, imposed

because of her body and its functions, in turn give her a different *psychic structure*, which, like her physiological
nature and her social roles, is seen to be closer to nature.
(Ortner, 1974:73-74).

All these factors combine to confine women to the context of the domestic family, and this confinement, particularly with its close association
with 'uncultured' children, reinforces the conception of women as further
removed than men from the cultural sphere.

The first difficulty in this analysis is that the argument is circular.
The assumption of the universality of this pattern is there at the outset.
When we are dealing with categorisations at the symbolic level, such as
sacred and profane, pure and impure, culture and nature, we are dealing
with forms of imagery which exist in particular contexts. Depending on
other factors, these forms of imagery can, when applied to categories of
individuals, result in completely different social statuses.

Another problem in this conceptualisation is the invariance which is
attributed to the social construction of biological difference. This type of
theory ultimately comes down to a disability thesis—the universal fact of
women's childbearing capacity is seen to be a cause of women's subordination, which we now have the means to overcome. Firestone's thesis is
thus not as different from the others as it may at first appear. The only
difference is that in the model set up by Ortner, a 'power psychology' is
not attributed to males. Both approaches share the assumption that
women's reproductive capacity lies at the basis of their devaluation.
However, the solutions proposed by those who argue this position are at
odds with each other. The radical feminists argue that changes will only
occur *despite* the desires of men, whereas those arguing as Ortner does
use a persuasion argument: that the technological means are at our disposal and women must argue for their application to particular obstacles
which they have faced as a result of their reproductive role.

A further problem with the approach epitomised by Ortner is that
women are viewed as passive recipients of a cultural definition of themselves imposed by males: 'she accepts her own devaluation and takes culture's point of view; (Ortner, 1974:76). No theory is adequate which
seeks to explain women's subordination without pursuing the reality of
their being active in defining themselves, and their relationships to
males.

I am not going to comment on whether women are necessarily subordinate to men in societies which symbolise sets of relationships along
the lines of male:female::public:private. But where it does exist as part of
a complex repertoire of symbolic representations, we need to establish

what relationships these have to 'social reality' and to the power embedded in relationships between people. I will say, though, that if this is the symbolism in a society where social production has been substantially removed from the household, then the notion of the private is an excluding one. While the main occupant of the 'private domain' is woman, in association with other marginal people—children (again, a recent historical phenomenon, rather than a universal one) then, since she is also involved in social production, her status in the latter domain is ambiguous. The most important point to keep in mind is that this is not an effect of biological differences but is an aspect of the economic mode of production broadly conceived. It is an historically accumulated effect of material practices, the most significant being the social/sexual division of labour and its pre-capitalist roots.

Marxist-feminist and related approaches

Here it is important to detail the role of Marxist-feminist theory in the general use of the public/private conceptualisation. The basis for this discussion will be an examination of Eli Zaretsky's *Capitalism, the Family and Personal Life* 1973 (1976). This is chosen because it is the best known example of such an approach. It has been very influential and widely read as an article (1973) and was reissued in book form three years after its first publication. It is addressed to understanding the ways in which this ideology of separation perpetuates women's subordination and considers much of the feminist literature as well as drawing on historical material.

Zaretsky argues that patriarchal ideology is vital in the reproduction of capitalism and, further, that the illusion of a private sphere where 'personal life' is created is an integral part of this ideology. This introduces an entirely new factor: the concept of a 'personal life', a subjectivity that is self-consciously seeking personal fulfilment. This has not been a factor in the analyses of non-capitalist modes of production. Indeed, one of Zaretsky's arguments is that this search is specific to capitalism.

He argues that public and private spheres are not universally conceived as separate: only under capitalism is it the case. This is how the economic role of the family is obscured. He also argues that the idea of the family as *the* arena for personal fulfilment contributes to women's subordination. He looks at the historically specific nature of this conceptualisation and how it has been transformed in various ways as the capitalist mode of production has developed to its current 'advanced' state.

Zaretsky has two main arguments. The first is that the rise of indus-

trial capitalism promoted a new search for personal identity outside the
social division of labour (1976:9). The second is that the expansion of this
'personal life' beyond the place of work created a new basis for women's
oppression, since the responsibility for maintaining a refuge from an
impersonal society was given to women, or at least to wives and mothers
(1976:10).

'Private' seems to be used in Zaretsky's account in two different ways.
He traces the separation of the family from the 'economy': with the
decline of the patriarchal family based upon private productive property,
there was a split between the socialised labour of the capitalist enterprise, and the home. The other process he explores is the increasing split-
ting off of people's personal lives from their place within the social division of labour. So 'private' refers at the same time to the home, and to
'inner being'. The distinction is an important one, as we shall see in looking at the different experiences of the family for men and for women.

Zaretsky traces the particular process of the proletarianisation of the
petty bourgeoisie, which gave rise to a need for a search for personal
identity outside the sphere of work. This became increasingly so as capitalism required a rationalised labour process 'undisturbed by community
sentiment, family responsibilities, personal relations and feelings'
(1976:47–8). This in time led to a new ideology of the family, seen as an
enclave which served to protect the emotional needs of its members.
Women were firmly placed inside this enclave and it was their role to
nurture within the family the 'human' values crushed by modern life. By
the second half of the nineteenth century, a contrast was formulated
between what was regarded as human/natural and divine on the one
hand and the profanity and rationality of 'society' on the other. Women
were associated with what is natural and human, as opposed to the
'unnatural' monster (society) that had been created through industrialisation. Of course, only women within families were regarded in this way:
women who had to work, or women in the public streets, were on the profane side of the equation and provided more reason to keep 'pure' women
away from public life.

Here the compounding effects of class and gender are particularly evident, in terms of the production of different forms of masculinity and
femininity at different class locations. The process which began at the
end of the seventeenth century and became elaborated during the nineteenth, promoted the idea of the purity and cleanliness of women
(Davidoff, 1976:122) and coincided with the disruptive effects of early
capitalism in England. Working-class men had considerable power over
their female counterparts in this respect. While working-class women

were occupied in performing the 'dirty' tasks for middle-class women–as 'domestic servants, washerwomen, charwomen—or prostitutes', working-class men remained true to both their masculine *and* class position:

> manual work and hence dirt, or the absence of cleanliness became associated with ideas of masculinity. Personal habits associated with dirt and mess, e.g. spitting, chewing tobacco and smoking, became strictly masculine from the end of the eighteenth century onwards. Similar attitudes were part of an aggressively proletarian identification. (Davidoff, 1976:129)

With the decline of the family based on individual private property and the increasing proletarianisation of the petty bourgeoisie, it was acknowledged that one's individual identity could no longer be realised through work or the ownership of property. The family was given new emphasis as the arena within which individuals could 'be themselves' and be valued for themselves. Zaretsky traces this process particularly in relation to the bourgeoisie, showing how the bourgeois ideology of individualism and its connection with the capitalist enterprise changed the meaning of the relationship between work and home (see also Davidoff, 1976, and her reasons for examining the middle-class household with servants). As the ideology of women's place in the home gained momentum, and as educational institutions were created for training young children, childhood and motherhood also changed in status. Zaretsky makes the point that it was not only the wage labourer who emerged with the capitalist system, but also the 'housewife' and her particular role in relation to the emotional well-being of her husband and her children (1976:64). Zaretsky argues from this that the development of the new ideal of the family obscured two things: the changes in the form of patriarchal ideology, and the subsuming under class relations both women's oppression and the family (1976:44).

There are several problems with this account. The most fundamental lies in the implication that class relations were primary and that the particular ways in which women's oppression were manifested was a secondary outcome. As should be clear from the preceding few pages, the constitution and constant re-formation of class boundaries and relationships were bound up, in a way that cannot be separated out, with the forms of employment (or non-employment) of the men and women of the different classes. We can historically situate the symbolic representation of the association of women with purity and cleanliness and men with impurity, dirt and manual labour, while we recognise at the same time that these categories were also predominantly attributed to classes, to both males and females:

> Even more important than the equation of femininity with cleanliness, was, of course, the equation of cleanliness with class position, part of the parcel of behaviour and attitudes bundled together in that imprecise but vital concept *respectability* . . . In the nineteenth century the labouring classes, the poor, the proletariat were, in middle-class minds, 'The Great Unwashed'; they *smelled* uncontrolled and disordered. (Davidoff, 1976:129)

We should not be surprised to find these contradictions, nor that the net effect of them was a hierarchical system by which the most powerful category—the bourgeois male—was ambiguously defined: masculine (dirty) but middle-class (clean). As Davidoff points out, it is a symbol of power to have subordinates protect you from the impurities of the world (or of yourself). At the bottom of the hierarchy, of course, is the working-class woman, subjected both to masculine domination and class servitude, also ambiguously defined, in her relationship to the masculine category of dirt.[2] But in this case, the ambiguity compounded her powerlessness. The outcome was in accord with the interests of the most dominant and powerful social group—the males of the bourgeoisie. The point, though, is to indicate that class formation did not *subsume* women's oppression. Women's work and the definitions of their places were integral to the processes of class formation. They were also integral to the definitions of masculinity and femininity, within different classes.

Another problem with Zaretsky's account is the uncritical assumption that the family is not only a haven or retreat for the man within it, but is *the* arena for personal fulfilment for fathers and husbands. As they see it, this is at the expense of the mothers and wives. Both of these assumptions need to be examined more closely.

It is unclear from Zaretsky's account whether he sees the idea of the family as 'haven' among the proletariat as simply the permeation of the bourgeois ideal of family life. If so, this would be in line with other writers' understanding of class hegemony. As Connell and Irving define it, it is 'a situation where the subordinate class lives its daily life in forms created by, or consistent with the interests of, the dominant class, and through this daily life acquires beliefs, motives, and ways of thinking that serve to perpetuate the class structure' (1980:22). This perspective can err towards the assumption of a passive acceptance by the working class of the 'lifestyles' and habits and preferences that perfectly suit the dominant class. Zaretsky comments: 'The rise of "mass consumption" has vastly extended the range of "personal" experience available to men and women while retaining it within an abstract and passive mode: the purchase and consumption of commodities' (1976:68).

Zaretsky suggests another reinforcing aspect: that the separation of personal lives from work lives creates a need on the part of the proletariat for a search for personal fulfilment. Zaretsky is careful to point out that this process is constructed somewhat out of the hands of the individuals in pursuit of this happiness, but he supplies no evidence for this being a new need, nor that it was successful. He seems to be claiming that people do experience this and, furthermore, that it is situated precisely within the family: 'the development of a separate sphere of personal life means that sections of the modern working class have a real sphere of personal freedom and independence which previous labouring classes did not have, and this sphere has increased as capitalism has developed' (1976:138). He is aware that this does not apply to women, for whom the family is also a place of work, and that there is no refuge from this to which they can escape. But there is evidence—from both 'middle-class' and working-class families—that even for men, a refuge, an escape from alienating circumstances, does not necessarily exist within the family.

Zaretsky indicates the contradictions involved in the family *experienced* as a 'haven': 'Under capitalism almost all our personal needs are restricted to the family. This is what gives the family its resilience . . . and this also explains its inner torment; it simply cannot meet the pressure of being the only refuge in a brutal society' (1976:140-1).

Zaretsky lacks conceptual clarity. What he means by 'personal life' is variously described as: private, the inner world, inner life, personal life, inner emotional life, and intimate personal experience. The family is described both as utopian retreat and the domestic sphere. These are simply not all expressions of the same thing. Similarly, his use of the word 'subjectivity' is explained as 'the search for personal identity outside the social division of labour' (1976:34). This is not satisfactory in the light of the various ways in which the 'subjective' element of social life can be formulated.

We have evidence from Bott (1957), Seeley, Sim and Loosley (1963), Sennett and Cobb (1973) and from other research that the family may not be the central arena for the personal fulfilment of its members.[3] The family means different things to different people, not only in different social classes and historical periods, but also in relation to the occupational experiences of its members. For instance, Seeley and his associates make it clear that 'fulfilment' and 'personal identity' can be sought in the

domain of work: the family may simply be an essential backup service for
this process. In relation to the upper middle-class families they described,
they say:

> The male occupational role demands concentration upon
> rationalistic competition and efficiency, with progress
> gauged by profits or similar objective evidences. Personal
> relationships, *even within the family* may be limited,
> impersonal, or pseudo-personal, directed towards specific
> ends. Thus the family may be used primarily to promote the
> career. (1963:177, my emphasis)

Some of the men in this sample looked upon the family as an 'emotionally
safe refuge [and] for this very reason *refused to become deeply involved
with the members of their families*. They needed protection against dis-
turbance, and so chose a life of non-involvement' (my emphasis).

The work of Sennett and Cobb (1973) presents a similar picture for
working-class men, although the situations of the men are quite different. The work and family connection is not the same. The 'performance
principle', as Marcuse (1972a) refers to it, is so deeply ingrained in the
belief structure of the Boston workers whom Sennett and Cobb interviewed that their sense of failure in the occupational sphere does not
allow them to believe that they are *justified* in any pursuit of fulfilment
for themselves. Whereas Zaretsky claims that there has been 'the rise of
a new emphasis on personal life, experienced as something outside work
and society' (1976:9), the Boston men refuse to accept this for themselves. Even for their children they are concerned less with personal fulfilment than with occupational success. That is, they are ambivalent
about pushing their children in the direction of jobs with perhaps less
intrinsic satisfaction than their own but with more status and security.
They recognise the ambiguities in the situation and feel them more profoundly than the word 'dilemma' conveys.

Research carried out on industrial workers seems to provide a better
basis for an understanding of 'personal life'. Zaretsky stresses the radical
feminist emphasis on personal relationships and the demand for their
complete transformation. These sorts of calls from the radical political
movements led, during the 1960s in particular, to an emphasis on the
importance of personal lives. From this, Zaretsky deduces that this was a
felt need on the part of sections of the working class at least, and one
they actively created: '[T]he contemporary proletariat, having no private
property to uphold, upholds the "self" as an autonomous realm outside

society. The idea of "life-style" expresses this ideology' (1976:143).

It seems clear that Zaretsky's exclusive association of personal life with the family needs to be modified by the empirical data we do have: data in relation to second jobs, overtime, separate friendship ties of husband and wife, mateship, the future orientation of the parents in relation to their children, the 'different marriages' which are experienced by husband and wife within the same marriage (Bernard, 1976) and so on.

The proletariat to which Zaretsky refers needs to be viewed, not as passive recipients of a bourgeois ideal but as individuals, who sometimes painfully, but actively, attempt to construct their present and future reality. The constraints expressed in the concept of hegemony certainly operate. But within this structured reality, of particular interest are the ways in which categories of people systematically choose to reject or resist or reinterpret for themselves their place in the social world. What requires explanation, then, are the ways in which categories of workers think that they are carving out 'individual' solutions to their problems, but in fact are constructing these in the same way as others similarly situated in the class structure.

In sum, although Zaretsky recognises the connection between 'personal life' and the capitalist mode of production, and the ways in which the latter 'mass-produces' the former, he nevertheless maintains a degree of separation by describing a personal sphere as if it were necessarily experienced as a reasonably relaxed and pleasant place. In contrast, Mitchell points out that

> [t]he belief that the family provides an impregnable enclave of intimacy and security in an atomized and chaotic cosmos assumes the absurd—that the family can be isolated from the community, and that its internal relations will not reproduce *in their own terms* the external relations which dominate the society. The family as a refuge from society in fact becomes a reflection of it. (1971:146-7)

It is also a distortion of the wider society. These paradoxes have important implications for the ways in which time spent outside the production process is dealt with. It may not be a 'personal' arena at all.

The male wage labourer

This section is concerned with the work of Goldthorpe, Lockwood and associates,[4] and of Sennett and Cobb (1973), all of which is directed towards male industrial workers' images of the class society within which they live and the impact of these on attitudes towards work and family life. I have two main purposes here: first, to indicate the inadequacies of much research that assumes workers are generally male, and which interprets its findings accordingly. Second, I wish to point to methodological issues which throw light on the different conclusions reached by the two sets of researchers in so far as a public/private distinction is or is not attributed to the world views of the people being investigated.

Goldthorpe and associates developed their main thesis of the 'privatised' worker between 1963 and 1972 in response to a prevailing conception in Western social and political thought that increasing affluence was making the working class similar in important respects to the 'middle class'. In terms of income, lifestyle, political and industrial attitudes, it was argued, a process of 'embourgeoisement' was occurring, and would continue.

In the introduction to their final book in the *Affluent Worker* series (1969)[5] Goldthorpe and associates suggest an alternative interpretation for the changes that were occurring in the working class at the time; this involved three related concepts. The first is the need to consider the new, *pecuniary* model of society held by some members of the working class. Rather than viewing the social world in terms of differences of power, or of status, these workers see money, and what it can buy, as the main difference between categories of people.[6]

Second, in the authors' view, this attitude is confirmed by an increasing tendency for workers to choose their jobs not for the intrinsic satisfaction they provide but for economic rewards: 'work was defined and experienced essentially as a means to the pursuit of ends outside of work and usually ones relating to standards of domestic living' (Goldthorpe et al., 1969:164).

This leads to a third related concept: the *privatised* worker. The privatised worker sees his future as centred on home, which has to do with rising standards of living. This also has day-to-day consequences 'manifested in a pattern of social life which is centred on, and indeed largely restricted to, the home and the conjugal family' (Goldthorpe et al., 1969:97). They concentrate on a particular segment of the working class, chosen precisely because its attitude to the domestic sphere differs from that of the 'traditional' working class. However, they suggest that its manifestation may be more widespread (1969:164).

Some elaboration of these three related concepts is necessary to indicate how tenuous the links between them are. Privatisation has several meanings attached to it, none of which are necessarily related. The first is the male workers' home-centredness just mentioned. This is explained partly as a concern to spend time with the family, and partly as an over-riding desire to accumulate consumer durables and other material posses-sions which they and their families can enjoy. Privatisation is also explained by the infrequency of social contacts outside the family, and the time spent in home-centred activities.

This private way of life meshes in with the emphasis placed on the wage, which 'buys' the way of life. Work is important only for its *extrin-sic* value; it is devalued except as a means to higher consumption. As Goldthorpe sees it, this is borne out by the scant interest in seeking promotion,[7] or success in occupational terms, by the limited social inter-actions among the workers outside work hours, and by the readiness of many of the migrants to Luton[8] they surveyed to accept lower job pres-tige in order to be paid more.

The main points to extract from these authors' research are these. First, there is an absolute distinction made between work life and home life. The only connection between them is the wage. Second, possessions are defined in a broad sense and include intangible possessions, the most important one in this account being the education that money can buy, 'a possession that enables one to earn more money' (Lockwood, 1975:24). Third, these workers' aspirations were conceived only in terms of 'ones relating to steadily increasing consumer capacity and to yet higher material standards of life' (Goldthorpe et al., 1969:39). Fourth, the pic-ture drawn of family life included an assumption of 'a more "companion-ate" or partnership-like form' and that, consequently, 'relations both between husband and wife and between parents and children would seem likely to become closer and more inherently rewarding' (Goldthorpe et al., 1968b:175). This assumption is based on the premise that, if workers are 'better able to satisfy their expressive and affective needs through family relationships', they are less likely to seek a work milieu in which satisfactions of this kind can be met. Finally, and this is related to their refutation of the embourgeoisement thesis, these workers are not con-cerned to be categorised as middle-class, and in fact 'attitudes towards middle-class persons are often critical (e.g. in regard to their anxiety over "keeping up appearances" and "class distinctions", and their "preten-sions" to gentility)' (1969:25).

Goldthorpe's and Lockwood's idea of the privatised worker can really only be applied to *male* privatised workers. It was not applied to women in their sample, even though many of them worked, and nor could it be, since the links between family and work for them could not be analysed only in terms of the wage: childcare and domestic responsibilities, as well as prevailing attitudes towards women working, intervene. As has been shown, their thesis can hardly be sustained in relation to males and it was not designed to apply to females. The whole analysis precluded them; Lockwood's typology of the working class—traditional, deferential, and privatised (1975)—refers only to males.

Whereas Goldthorpe and Lockwood stress the immediate pleasure of consumption, leisure and family relationships, Sennett and Cobb stress the sacrificial nature of the male's occupational role, the associated sacrifices by the wife, and the tensions and resentments between husband and wife and parents and children that these sacrificial relationships engender. They also stress that, as a result, the worker's response to his position in society is ambivalent.

Rather than conducting interviews, Sennett and Cobb held 'intensive and probing conversations' (1973:9) with a group of male workers and their families in Boston. They saw themselves as urban anthropologists, as participant observers in schools, bars, and people's homes. They had no rigid questionnaire, rather 'a set of concerns we wanted to explore' (1973:41). In contrast to Goldthorpe's and Lockwood's interpretation, they say:

> The activities which keep people moving in a class society, which makes them seek more money, more possessions, higher-status jobs, do not originate in a materialistic desire, or even sensuous appreciation, of things, but out of an attempt to restore a psychological deprivation that the class structure has effected in their lives. In other words, *the psychological motivation instilled by a class society is to heal a doubt about the self rather than create more power over things and other persons in the outer world* (1973:171)

Sennett and Cobb argue that for a man a job means that he can give his children enough money and a sufficiently stable home for them to obtain a good education and move into a higher class. He thinks of himself as a sacrificer and uses this to oppress his wife and children. To the extent that work gives him a sense of worth, it is because it involves sacrifices in relation both to his own satisfactions and to the time he has left to spend with his family.

Goldthorpe and Lockwood see people spending most of their lives working without satisfaction, but gaining their contentment within the family; for the men Sennett and Cobb spoke to, there is no contentment in either sphere. First, the man rarely spends as much time as he would like with his family (1973:48); second, he cannot, in his own lifetime, erase the tensions engendered by this sacrificial contract.

It should not be concluded that these differences in responses are attributable to different social and historical situations. There are, in fact, some significant similarities in the two sets of research, which suggest that the apparent differences have more to do with the interpretations made by the researchers and the methods they employed.

One striking similarity between these groups of workers is their lack of occupational ambition for themselves. Their concern is rather for their family and its future, as expressed, at least in part, by their ability to afford educational opportunities for their children, so that they will move into more satisfying jobs. Both sets of researchers refer to the dilemma about job satisfaction and money that has confronted these workers, and to their desire to elevate their children out of it.

This points to another dilemma which is clearly formulated in Sennett's and Cobb's work. While the men wanted their children to have better lives than they had experienced themselves, they had little respect for the sort of occupations those better lives might involve, which they regarded as middle-class. This ambivalence—wanting to push one's children up into the category of people for whom one felt both envy and lack of respect—is not explored by Goldthorpe and Lockwood.

What is equally clear is that parents' expectations are generally ill-founded. As Goldthorpe and Lockwood comment,

> the discrepancy between parental aspirations and children's performance is often quite striking. For instance, more than 6 out of 10 of the couples we interviewed expressed a preference for grammar school education, but so far less than 1 child out of 10 has achieved this. Again, half the couples wanted to see their sons in white-collar jobs and only a quarter limited their aspirations to manual work; yet among those of their sons who have entered the labour market, under a fifth have secured white-collar employment and manual work is the lot of three-quarters. (1969:135–6)

Sennett and Cobb make the same point (1973:187).

Goldthorpe and Lockwood deal with why there might be a discrepancy between aspirations and fulfilment in terms of the differential resources of manual workers as against middle-class parents as regards their children's education. They do not look at the results of thwarted ambitions. They simply reassert their original premise: that there is a category of the working class for whom neither power nor status models of society operate: for these workers, education for more money is of primary significance.

If a 'pecuniary' model of society does indeed prevail in workers' minds, it is not enough to say merely that the family has become the focus of strivings for personal satisfaction. What has to be asked is whether these strivings are successful. If not, what effect does this have on relationships within the family, and on attitudes to education and to work? What are the consequences of thwarted aspirations for children, or unfulfilled desires for material possessions? How can such failures be repeated and accepted by successive generations? How do people accept that all their efforts are likely to be in vain?

Sennett and Cobb provide some answers to these questions. While the workers they spoke to indicate disrespect for the middle class and are consequently ambivalent about what they want for their children, they recognise that power is an intangible quality which middle-class individuals possess, and which they in turn feel they can, through sacrifices, give to their children. So power is integral to their view of the world, rather than some combination of power, status and money models. As well as this, they are actively creating a present and a future for themselves, rather than placing prime importance on consumption per se. Sennett and Cobb point out that these people

> were determined that, if circumstances of class had limited their freedom in comparison to that of educated people, they would *create* freedom for themselves . . . they were resolved to shape the actions open to them so that, in their own minds, *they felt as though they acted from choice rather than necessity*. (1973:121, latter emphasis mine)

This suggests a reappraisal of the 'pecuniary' model. Westergaard correctly points out that it is not plausible to

> draw a sharp line of division between home and work as rival centres of 'life interest' and social consciousness. If the wage packet increasingly is the only link that ties the worker to a grudging commitment to his work, to his bosses, and to society at large, that is a brittle strand, liable to wear thin or to snap when the dependability of earnings is threatened or pay rises fail to keep pace with rising demands. (Westergaard, 1972:162)

The results of both sets of research make it possible to question the assumption of the separation of spheres. In both samples, more manual workers than non-manual workers worked either overtime or at two jobs (Sennett and Cobb, 1973:99; Goldthorpe et al., 1969:98). And in both surveys, the wives of manual workers were less likely to work than the wives of non-manual workers (Sennett and Cobb, 1973:99; Goldthorpe et al.,

1969:37). This immediately throws into question the validity of the 'pecuniary' model as it has been presented. The husband-father expresses resistance to the idea of his wife seeking paid employment even when her employment would raise the family's income level. This creates an intervening factor.

The Boston worker expresses the paradox in terms of his own life-history: though anxious not to be the absent father of his childhood experience (Sennett and Cobb, 1973:123), he makes this inevitable by insisting that his wife should not go out to work. He plays the part of sacrificial provider. This is, however, increasingly untenable and in recent years economic necessity has forced more married women to work and thus share the 'sacrificial pact' with their husbands (Sennett, 1978).[9]

Goldthorpe and Lockwood attribute the difference in the proportion of wives working in their manual and non-manual samples to two things: the difficulties of working around shift work and overtime, and the fact that the manual workers' families tend to have more children. This interpretation is open to dispute: as far as the second point is concerned, fertility rates could quite as easily be a function of the fact that the wife does not work.

The assumption is made in this research that the lower fertility rates of white-collar wives (a trend which is now in reverse, conceivably for the economic reasons outlined here) enable them to work in greater numbers than the manual workers' wives. However, many other things need to be considered: for example, the lower fertility rates may reflect a greater desire on the part of these women to work, or less resistance on the part of their husbands. This latter possibility was certainly the case in Sennett's earlier investigation (1970:124). Here, increased income was sacrificed for emotional stability in the manual worker's home, by not challenging the authority patterns since, had the wife worked, it would have been in a white-collar job, paying better than the husband's job. In the Boston sample, there was a resistance expressed on the part of the husbands, one which some of the wives expressed resentment about (Sennett and Cobb, 1973:129). Similarly, the higher fertility rates among the manual workers cannot only be seen in terms of explaining their lesser likelihood to work. Again, it might be a reflection of the man's idea of his role as breadwinner; it would certainly not be unrelated to the fact that the men in this category are at their peak earning capacity in their early years of marriage, whereas the white-collar men can look forward to greater economic returns later (Goldthorpe et al., 1969:127-9). Moreover, the greater likelihood of the male taking on overtime (up to fifteen hours a week) cannot be interpreted purely in terms of the extra gains in income; it needs to be assessed in relation to attitudes towards women working as well as the emphasis placed on spending time with the family.

These work patterns—shift work and overtime—throw into question the basic thesis which Goldthorpe and Lockwood present. Sennett and Cobb make clear the irony of the situation where the man cannot enjoy family life because he is so preoccupied with providing for his family. This is not explored in Goldthorpe's and Lockwood's work. The tables they present of typical evenings and weekends for four of their couples—presented to indicate the home-centredness of their activities—indicate not only the time spent away from the family by the adult male, but the *separate* home-centred activities of the husband and wife (1969:99–101).

'Privatisation', then, is conceptually confusing. There is no evidence that the associated 'pecuniary' ideology has led to more harmonious family relationships. Komarovsky (1964:336) suggests, from her own research findings, that the ideal of companionship deepens the sense of inadequacy of husbands and wives who know they 'should talk to one another, but . . . find nothing to say'. It certainly does seem to imply, in this particular sample, a cutting off of family units from each other. But while Goldthorpe and Lockwood argue that this cutting off is a preference, and a satisfying one, it would appear equally plausible to argue that it results from lack of time.

Conclusions

I would argue that much feminist theory has been uncritical by assuming that the male necessarily benefits from an institution that has been described as a major source of unhappiness and strain for women. Feminist theory simply has to take account of the possibility that Sennett and Cobb, and Goldthorpe and associates, are correct about the inability of these people to change the life chances of their children. Further, if Sennett and Cobb are correct in saying that male dominance in the working-class family is partly based on sacrifice to this end, then feminist theory must concern itself with these patterns. In other words, the class as against the personal nature of the male's lack of self-esteem must be dealt with in the same way that feminist theory has so effectively pointed to the social rather than the personal nature of the female's lack of self-esteem, and the female's objective lack of power to define her own life in many respects. Concentrating only on the latter will not change the basis for male dominance if, as Sennett and Cobb indicate, this is closely related to work experience and the dominant ideology of individualism and achievement.

The concept of 'privacy', and its particular manifestation in nuclear households, allows for the acting out of familial relationships unhindered by observers, whether kin, neighbours, or other acquaintances (see Laslett, 1974). It also enables the *idea* of the family as haven and retreat, the site for love and affection within which one could be 'oneself', to really take root. But, as many commentators on the family indicate, one cannot assume this to be the reality. Barrington Moore, in the context of a wider critique of conventional notions of the family, gives one example: 'One absolutely un-Bohemian couple I know agreed in the privacy of their own home that if people ever talked to each other openly about the sufferings brought on by raising a family today, the birth rate would drop to zero' (Moore, 1969:458). In a similar vein, Lee Comer points to the implications of the quiet playing out of antagonisms between the sexes within the confines of the family:

> The bridge that marriage constructs across the sexes is an illusion which most of us are constrained to enact as reality ... As long as men and women quarrel in private or submerge their differences in silence, while maintaining a married face to the outside world, the chasm between women and men will continue to serve the society that created it. (Comer, 1974:211)

Sennett and Cobb point to a psychology of oppression among the Boston workers. As far as research into the industrial worker is concerned, the links between family and work must be explored using research methods which *assume* a complex, even contradictory and ambivalent response to the social world. Feminist theory has effectively criticised the ideology of the family as a private, separate 'haven' for the woman within it, and is beginning to question the nature of the family as experienced by the adult male.[10] Working-class men are profoundly damaged by the effects of the class structure and patriarchal ideology on their work and their family lives. In many ways the family is an unpleasant place for everyone involved. The family or the household as a socially constructed space may be, at different times for different people, the site for personal fulfilment. It is other things as well. Similarly, work is experienced, among other things, as a place where one can be 'oneself' (Seeley et al., 1963; Willis, 1977). This underlies how unsatisfactory it is to equate public (or impersonal) with work, and private (personal) with home.

The material presented here suggests the need for modification of both the radical feminist position and the position taken by Zaretsky, promoting the idea that male members of the proletariat successfully sought personal fulfilment within the family. Sennett's and Cobb's material indicates how one's work experience might lead to a lack of a sense of worth, with important implications for the ways in which the 'personal' sphere is dealt with by men. These, of course, have effects on women and children who are drawn into their view of the world and the males' sacrificial bargains. Women are also affected at the workplace, as males' seeking of masculine ego-satisfaction is not restricted to the non-work sphere. The reorganisation of the labour process in ways that perpetuate, albeit in different form, gender divisions at work, similarly reflect protectionist strategies which allow for some assertion of masculine power (Burton, 1983; Game and Pringle, 1983).

4

Domestic labour and the political economy of women

> Housework produces no surplus value: that is a different con-
> dition from that of the worker who is robbed of the surplus
> value he produces. I want to know exactly what is the rela-
> tionship between the two. The whole strategy of the women's
> struggle should depend on that. (de Beauvoir, Interview in
> *Seven Days* 8 March 1972)

Man as worker, woman as domestic labourer: this is another version of
the distinction between 'public' and 'private', and one which has been
steadily eroded as the 'domestic labour debate' has developed.

One consequence of the close attention given to the family by feminist
theorists was that no clear distinction was made between questions about
the relation of the family to the wider capitalist system, and those about
the relation of women to capitalism. 'Domestic labour', broadly defined to
include all work done within the home by women, was the focus of
attempts to explain these connections.

The main contribution of this whole discussion has been the transfer
in emphasis from the family, seen at first as the crucial site of women's
subordinate status, to the relation between the paid and unpaid work of
women. It is the significance of this relationship for the maintenance of
the class structure, for the production of capitalist social relations that
emerged from the domestic labour debate as the central concern.[1]

In this chapter I shall trace the development of the arguments cen-
tring around women's unpaid work, and detail the context of the theoretical shifts that occurred. Australian theorists have made significant
contributions in this area and I pay particular attention to these.

There have been two theoretical concerns, as far as domestic labour
has been connected to capital: its economic and ideological implications.
Concern with ideology at first reflected the radical-feminist emphasis on

the common oppression of all women. Attention has since shifted to the particular manifestations of patriarchy in different classes, still seen, however, as integral parts of the ideological structure of capitalism.

The early concentration on the ideological aspects of work performed within the family involved two separate arguments. One, which could loosely be called a radical-feminist position, emphasised the importance of domestic labour in relation to the benefits accruing to all males. The second, a Marxist-feminist approach, emphasised the economic importance of the ideology of women's domestic place in an attempt to establish its connection with capitalism (see Morton, 1971).

More recent integration of these positions has relied on developments in other areas: for example, the empirical detailing of segmentation processes in the labour market, theories of the state, and accounts of legitimation processes. Further developments have been facilitated by empirical research into the relationship between the paid and unpaid labour of women, the recurrent booms and recessions of capitalism and the progress of class struggle. In the light of this latter work, some of the directions which had been taken while the domestic labour debate remained at an abstract, theoretical level proved to be misconceived.

An important development through these theories has been the claim that there are limits to capital's ability to socialise the work that is done within the family. This was first expressed in terms of the personal services provided by women: 'What institution could provide Capital with strike-breakers, appreciative sexual objects, self-denying ego-builders —just to mention some of the functions—all on a 24 hour basis, and at a minimal cost to Capital?' (Campioni et al., 1974b:11). Later, this work was defined strictly in terms of the necessity for the individual consumption of the labourer to occur outside the production day.

Previously, consumption was referred to in the context of the family as a consumption unit and the housewife as the main consumer (see Friedan, 1965). The later reference to the 'individual consumption of the labourer' means something entirely different. The reproduction of the process of production involves the reproduction, not only of the means of production, but of the wage labourer as well. His/her maintenance and reproduction is carried out by the replenishment of his/her labour-power from day to day, and also the replenishment of the labour force from generation to generation. The daily replenishment involves eating and sleeping and maintaining oneself as a fit and able worker, so that one can go to work the next day. This is what is meant by the 'individual consumption of the labourer' as distinct from the productive consumption of one's labour-power by capital in the process of production. The point is that domestic work lies outside the production process when narrowly defined, but since the reproduction of labour-power is necessary to production, domestic work must be seen as part of the process of production more broadly understood as including its own reproduction.

The early contributors to the debate failed to distinguish analytically the work performed from those who were performing it. If unpaid work in the home can be demonstrated to be an essential component of the capitalist system, attention needs to be addressed to the work itself. The fact that women have been culturally assigned to this work can then be assessed, with regard, first, to the ways in which women's domestic labour contributes to capital accumulation, and second, to the ways in which it is connected to patriarchal ideology as a legitimising aspect of capitalist social relations. These processes in later enquiries were found not to be independent of one another.

The genesis of the concern with housework can be pinpointed fairly precisely. An article was published in 1970 called 'The politics of housework' by Pat Mainardi. It was reproduced in many anthologies and was widely distributed in pamphlet form in Britain, America and Australia.[2] It is difficult, now, to understand why it went through so many reprintings and was so widely read and discussed. But it performed a very important role at the time. As Mainardi pointed out, to talk, or write, about housework seems so *trivial*. The article is not an analysis of the work but a description of the process of trying to share it with a man who, like herself, was employed full-time. It was a significant document, in that it gave feminists more confidence to begin the exploration of domestic tasks as *work*, and to examine the implications of the fact that, having been defined as women's work, it was trivialised.

It is a particular feature of capitalism that women perform two types of labour—social and privatised. It is interesting, then, that women's social labour was excluded from much of this early analysis. The distinction between economy and family was maintained, and women's work within the latter was analysed separately, with the implicit assumption that men occupied the other sphere.

While radical feminism with its theme of the common oppression of all women was dominant in feminist literature, and socialist feminists were reacting against conventional Marxist analyses of the family, a distinction between the family on the one hand, and the place of the housewife-mother within it on the other, did not develop. Though the woman rather than the family was the main concern, it was in the context of the latter that women as housewives and mothers were seen as sharing a common oppression. The arguments between radical feminists and

Marxist-feminists began from this shared proposition.

Radical-feminist positions have an important place in the sequence of theoretical developments. A crude and early version was argued in several articles in the book edited by Robin Morgan (1970) and by Betsy Warrior in *Notes from the Third Year* (1971) and later, with Lisa Leghorn, in the *Houseworkers' Handbook* (1974). This particular perspective argues that there are two classes of men—capitalist and wage-labourer—and all women are outside this categorisation. They are the more exploited for this reason, as all males benefit from their labour, and capitalist males benefit twice: '[M]en constitute an upper caste who have a monopoly on economic and political power' (Warrior, 1971:69). This is put more strongly:

> Women are the source of all labour in that they are the producers of all labourers. [Their labour] creates the first commodity, female and male labourers, who in turn create all other commodities and products. Men as the ruling class profit from this commodity through its labour. These profits come in two sizes: king-size and super. The individual man who is king of his castle (the patrilineal family) has his labour power produced, prepared and maintained for him free . . . The *male* capitalist class makes a super-profit when it buys this labour power and then receives the surplus value of its 'outside' economy production. (1971:70)

Women's primary oppression, then, lies in their role as unpaid domestic workers. This analysis implies that the benefits to male wage labourers entirely offset the disadvantages inherent in their class position. It points to one solution: the abolition of 'housework' as it is now known:

> This means that work that was formerly done in separate, duplicated, [*sic*] single units will be collectivized and industrialized on a large basis with a more efficient use of both time and labour and without the waste, alienation, and duplication [*sic*] now involved in child care and home maintenance. (Warrior, 1971:71)

Women, in this scheme, become *the* significant oppressed group. Sexual, rather than class, antagonism is primary. The institution of the family oppresses all women, regardless of class.

The form of the debate between radical feminists and Marxist-feminists was not merely an internal argument within the women's movement, but was conditioned by the existence of the 'male left'. The importance of domestic work was argued in terms of Marx's labour theory of value. Was domestic labour productive or unproductive in the sense in which Marx used these terms? It appeared important to establish this because of the political implications of the way in which women as domestic workers were to be categorised. This would situate women in the class structure and determine their ' "consciousness" or [their] "objective" revolutionary potential' (Fee, 1976:7).[3]

The debate about whether housework is, strictly speaking, productive developed as one aspect of a wider discussion of what Marx meant generally by the terms 'productive' and 'unproductive'.[4] A great deal of this discussion does not deal specifically with housework, though several contributors pay some attention to the subject, partly as illustration, and partly as a result of work by feminists in Britain which appeared to merit consideration—if only to be dismissed. The relevance to the development of feminist theory was seen to lie in its contribution first to the definition of the class position of women and consequently of appropriate political action and second to groups of activists who were developing a strategy of 'wages for housework'.

Interaction with the 'male left' also contributed to the debate. Marxist-feminists were not in agreement with each other on this issue, but one approach was, in a sense, to make respectable the emotive, non-technical arguments of the radical feminists. By arguing that domestic work was productive, in the sense of contributing to surplus value, those who followed this line could then point to the failure of orthodox Marxist theory to take account of domestic production. In this view women's work in the home needed to be fully incorporated into the analyses of the process of capitalist production.

Women as a structural group

The first paper to argue that all women as domestic workers were exploited as a group was Benston's, 'The Political Economy of Women's Liberation, (1969). Benston argued that 'women as a group do indeed have a definite relation to the means of production and that this is different from that of men' (1969:13). The factors usually referred to in relation to women's oppression—personal and psychological factors—she saw as following from this special relation to production. Benston was concerned to construct a structural definition of women, such as that provided for wage labourers within Marxist analyses. She sought a 'statement of the material conditions in capitalist (and other) societies which define the group "women"' (1969:14). Benston defines this special position by reference to the fact that women are responsible for the 'production of use-values' within the family, as contrasted with and connected to commodity production, in which wage earners are involved, and on which the consumption within families is based (1969:16).

Benston recognised the family as a unit of consumption but did not see this as its prime characteristic; neither did she see the housewife chiefly as a consumer. Rather, she emphasised the other aspect of the family: as a productive unit for housework and childrearing:

> [E]ach family, each household, constitutes an individual production unit, a pre-industrial entity, in the same way that peasant farmers or cottage weavers constitute pre-industrial production units. The main features are clear, with the reduplicative, kin-based, private nature of the work being the most important. (1969:18)

This last quotation gives some clue to how the argument developed after her paper. It allows for the assertion that the household constitutes a separate mode of production. It also allows the argument already referred to, that housework needs to be analysed as productive labour. Benston's paper was used as a support for variations on each of these positions.

The publication of Dalla Costa's article 'The Power of Women and the Subversion of the Community' (1973) had a profound impact on the feminist movement. It was invoked in support of completely opposing points of view; it seemed to have something to offer to everyone. It was undoubtedly the most widely read and discussed of all the papers written on this subject and was constantly referred to as the debate proceeded. It also prompted responses from Marxists outside the women's movement (see Harrison, 1973b; Seccombe, 1974).

There are two main themes in this paper. The first is that domestic work is 'essential to the production of surplus value' (1973:31). The second is a rejection of the idea that entering the paid workforce is a solution to the problem of women. It argues firmly that the family is the arena for political struggle.

The way in which Dalla Costa dealt with the first theme brought some relief to those feminists who, until the publication of this paper, had been concerned to itemise separately the economic and ideological 'functions' of the family. The former tended to be listed in terms of the tangible work that housewives do in the service of husbands and children: cooking, washing, ironing, cleaning and so on. In Marxist terminology, this was generalised as the maintenance and reproduction of labour-power and the transformation of commodities into consumable form. This left the ideological functions somewhat at a loose end, since the purpose of the analyses was to indicate that the *totality* of women's work was of benefit to capital. Dalla Costa broke down this distinction by referring to the 'productivity of passivity' and the 'productivity of discipline' in relation to the repression of sexuality and the formation of the female personality on the one hand and the socialisation of children on the other (1973:40, 45). By doing this, Dalla Costa added a dimension to the 'economic' contribution of the family: the reproduction of relations of domination and subordination were related directly to capital accumulation. She included the reproduction of the social relations of production within the category of *productive* labour.

The other main theme was never taken up on a wide scale within the women's movement by activists, nor by theorists in the literature. That is, that women, rather than entering the paid labour force to be further subordinated to exploitative work relationships, should refuse to perform the domestic work which is the basis for their exploitation.[5] Hence, all women must organise separately from men: '[T]he specific form of exploitation represented by domestic work demands a corresponding, specific form of struggle, namely the woman's struggle, *within the family*' (Dalla Costa, 1973:33). The 'social factory' is the community and the family. Dalla Costa believes that the apparent 'privacy' of the work of housewives implies no limitation of opportunity for political struggle.

Even though it was explicitly rejected in Dalla Costa's text (1973:34), this position was congenial to the 'wages for housework' campaign which was associated with several groups in Great Britain, Canada and the United States. The influence of Selma James was instrumental in this shift. James was a founding member of the Power of Women Collective in London, the group most committed to the idea of wages for housework. Dalla Costa's article was published with an introduction by James and there are substantial modifications in footnotes written jointly by Dalla Costa and James for the edition distributed outside Italy. There is a note to the effect that changed economic circumstances made the strategy of wages for housework more feasible at the time of the English edition than it had been a year before, either in Italy or elsewhere (1973:52).

Both the articles by Benston and Dalla Costa precipitated an intensive and prolonged discussion about whether it could be argued that a separate, or client, domestic mode of production existed in relation to the dominant, capitalist one.[6]

During the period 1972–75 most of the contributions to this debate argued that the fact that housework was commonly performed by women served to constitute women as a structural group. Whichever way this labour might be defined, it involved all women in a different relationship to the means of production from that of men. Such arguments necessarily rest on the premise that the domestic work of all women is not differentiated with regard to its function for capital, or, if it is, that this is less important than the fact that it is the primary source of women's oppression. The extent to which women's paid labour was taken into account varied.

This is where the definitional arguments took over from the substantive ones. The main problem was to define domestic work in relation to capital while continuing to see it as being outside capitalist social relations. All the positions taken on this issue were seen by the authors to be relevant to political action. How domestic labour is defined was believed to have clear strategic implications for the feminist movement.

The main assumption is that the position of women as housewives is more important than either the class position of their families or the question of whether they are employed in paid labour. Although neither Benston nor Dalla Costa argued the case for recognising a separate mode of production, suggestive segments of their texts were taken up for this purpose by others. Dalla Costa made a similar point to that of Benston when she described the working conditions of the housewife as 'precapitalist' (1973:26). In addition, Benston stressed the importance of women's work in the home as against their paid labour: 'Notice that women are not excluded from commodity production. Their participation in wage labour occurs but, as a group, they have no structural responsibility in this area and such participation is ordinarily regarded as transient' (1969:16).

The domestic mode of production

Vort-Ronald can be taken as a representative exponent of the thesis that there exists a separate domestic mode of production.[7] The Australian writer whose treatment of the question is most widely known, and most frequently criticised, she is concerned to explain both women's general subordination and 'the ways in which specific groups of women are affected by the divisions of capitalism' (1974:21).

She quotes Vogel (1973) with approval: 'In short, domestic labour is neither productive nor unproductive . . . women's productive activity in the family "does not fall under the capitalist mode of production" strictly defined' (Vort-Ronald, 1974:23). The common characteristic of women,

that of being domestic labourers, is significant: 'Thus women who perform domestic labour form a group whose labour is appropriated in a distinct way in capitalist society, in a mode of production whose social relations differ from those of capitalist production' (1974:23). This means
that an autonomous women's movement is necessary to represent 'the
oppression which women share as domestic labourers' (1974:24).

A similar argument was developed by Harrison in Britain (1973b) in
the context of a wider Marxist debate concerned with the definition of
'productive workers'. For him, it is only within the wage-labour–capital
relationship that productive labour is conceivable in the capitalist mode
of production. Harrison introduces the category of *non*-productive
labour, which includes that of housewives. He acknowledges that housework performs for capital the essential functions of maintenance and
reproduction of the labourer (1973b:50). But, in relation to the capitalist
mode, he will not allow that the work of the housewife can be regarded as
productive. He conceives of a distinct domestic mode of production
within which the labour of the housewife finds its proper theoretical
place, and in relation to which it is undoubtedly productive. This formulation of the matter has further implications. As the output of the domestic mode is essential to the dominant capitalist mode which could not
otherwise reproduce itself, it becomes necessary to distinguish the capitalist mode of production, as Harrison more narrowly defines it, from
the capitalist *system* as a whole. It also follows that

> [s]ince housework is performed outside of capitalist produc-
> tion relations the people who perform it do not belong to
> either of the classes that are the bearers of these relations.
> Housewives are neither proletarians nor capitalists; they
> form a distinct class. This means, of course, that a large
> number of people fall into two classes. Women who work for
> capital and also perform a substantial amount of housework
> are both proletarians and housewives. (1973b:50)

Harrison pays little attention to the political implications of his argument. The question of women's class consciousness belongs, for him, to
the women's movement. This rests, of course, on the assumption that
housework is exclusively women's work.

Both Vort-Ronald and Harrison assert that this work could, in
principle, be socialised. But there are differences in their approaches.
Harrison says:

> It is not true that capital *needs* housework in the sense that
> there is no other way in which the functions could be ful-

filled. All of the economic functions of housework could be
fulfilled under capitalist production relations. There is no
reason ... why the principle of laundrettes could not be
extended to capitalist creches, and if you like, brothels. A
system in which everyone works directly for capital and
there is no sex role distinction is perfectly conceivable. In
such a system there *need* be no oppression specific to
women. (1973b:51)

For Harrison, the subordination of women is a secondary phenomenon,
not integral or necessary to the capitalist mode of production. For Vort-
Ronald, the transformation of capitalist social relations would be necessary to change the relations between the sexes (1974:24), as women's subordination rests on a social/sexual division of labour which capitalism
requires. She acknowledges the intersection of class and sexual oppression, as opposed to Harrison's conception of them as somehow independent. But she goes no further than a statement to that effect: 'The liberation of women requires the abolition of the sexual division of labour. In
concrete terms, this means the socialisation of housework and childcare
so that they are performed by both sexes, and absolute equality for
women in the workforce' (1974:24).

Another contribution to this definitional argument, which received a
great deal of attention within the feminist movement in Australia, was a
collaborative work by Marxist-feminists, some of whom have since gone
on to develop their ideas in the fields of psychoanalysis and theories of
ideology (Campioni, 1976b; Jacka, 1977). This article, 'Opening the
floodgates: domestic labour and capitalist production' (Campioni, et al.,
1974b)[8] is a defence of Dalla Costa against the criticisms of Harrison
(1973b) and Seccombe (1974). Like Dalla Costa, it argues that women
constitute a class. The authors wanted to emphasise the economic importance of the 'immaterial use-values provided by the woman in her role as
wife and mother', such as 'the provision of a sphere of personal relations,
tension management, psychological and sexual satisfaction ... and the
socialisation of husband and children into controllable and competitive
conforming workers' (1974b:11). They rely heavily on Marxist theory,
including Marx's own work, to defend this position. The article was
written at a time in Australia when the feminist movement was engaged
in discussing the idea of wages for housework.

Their thesis is that women's domestic work is an integral part of the
capitalist mode of production. It is the 'major contribution to the production and reproduction of the labour power of the collective worker
required by capital' and the woman is '*indirectly productive* of surplus

value and is thereby exploited in the capitalist sense' (Campioni et al., 1974b:10). Introduction of the concept, 'indirectly productive', modifies Dalla Costa's argument. The authors use Marx's comments on commercial workers, not only as an analogy but to assert the validity of categorising domestic labour in this different way: 'women who labour as housewives are . . . indirectly productive, not in that they do not directly create value, but in that the value they create is only realised as surplus value in the products of the industrial sector' (Campioni et al., 1974a:14). The argument is a straightforward one. If women's domestic work can be seen to be of economic interest to capital, if, directly or indirectly, it is contributing to capital accumulation, then the work is productive and contributes to the creation of surplus value.

They criticise Harrison for trivialising the concept of mode of production by defining it as narrowly as he does. They indicate the confusion that arises if the concept of mode of production is used in such a restricted and static sense that its reproduction is taken for granted. Harrison confines capitalist production to the industrial sector so that processes essential to the reproduction of capital are relegated to other modes. What the authors of this paper do is expand the meaning of capitalist production to 'the economic instance of the CMP in the broad sense, [which] is composed of a number of spheres or sectors (industrial, domestic, commercial) between which there may be marginal differences in their work relations' (1974a:4).

Campioni and her associates argue that the categorisation of women as productive labourers has political implications 'because it is relevant in determining economic class position'. They qualify this by saying that even if women were unproductive labourers under capitalism as Seccombe proposes (1974), they would still be performing surplus labour. They quote Marx on commercial workers: 'He creates no direct surplus value, but adds to the capitalist's income by helping him to reduce the cost of realising surplus value, inasmuch as he performs partly unpaid labour' (Marx, *Capital* vol. 2, cited in Campioni et al., 1974b:12). The definition of productive labour is relevant to the class analysis of women because this gives them a 'determinant place in the social division of labour and [they] are thus exploited as a class in a determinate manner' (Campioni et al., 1974b:13).

At the economic level, the close identification of the class interests of husband and wife are acknowledged. So it is through the intervention of ideology that women are constituted as a class. This is critically important in terms of 'formulating strategy and tactics in the Women's Liberation movements . . . The dominance of the ideological unites women as a whole in that it situates all women as subordinate in a system of social relations based on their sexual oppression' (1974b:14). The analysis points to the necessity for an autonomous women's movement to represent the specific class interests of women, at the same time as the working-class struggle continues. This involves the authors in some difficulties with the category of 'bourgeois' women:

> 'It would appear that there is a contradiction [for bourgeois women] between their economic and their ideological class interests. However, insofar as their ideological oppression as women stems, structurally if not historically, from the economic exploitation of proletarian women in the domestic labour process, we would hold that it is in the ultimate objective interest of middle-class women to unite with proletarian women in the overthrow of the latter's economic exploitation. (1974b:14).

A difference is pointed to, between the oppression of bourgeois women and the exploitation of working-class women. It is only the latter who can contribute to the value of labour-power. How did apparently Marxist analyses, at this time, arrive at conclusions such as these? An understanding of the connection between class and patriarchy was being attempted. But it was limited by narrow conceptions both of the economic structure and of ideology. There were particular reasons for this, some theoretical, others having to do with the social context of the time. These latter were bound up with the existence of an autonomous women's movement and the need to provide it with a rationale, couched not only in terms of women's psychological oppression but in terms of political strategy. The theoretical context was Marxist theory, used as a framework within which women could be categorised as a separate, structural group. The need to organise separately from men flowed into theoretical constructs in a way that was later rejected by many feminists.

A summary of the main problems in theoretical positions which argue that a distinct domestic mode of production exists can now be presented.

As we have seen, to postulate a separate domestic mode of production is one way to handle the issue of whether domestic labour is productive or unproductive—in effect, by circumventing it. Those who represented domestic labour as part of a separate mode of production were faced with the further question of whether to conceive of women as constituting a class, distinct from the male capitalist and working classes. The concept of a domestic mode depended on a narrow conception of what constituted a mode of production. Only while its reproduction was regarded as secondary and not integral, could this conceptualisation appear valid. An analogy between the household under capitalism and the subsistence work which is performed by women in social formations where there could be said to be a dominant, capitalist mode and a subordinate, non-capitalist mode is often made in the literature (O'Laughlin, 1975; Deere, 1976; Fee, 1976). This tends to result in another version of the public/private dichotomy: women being concerned with the production of use-values, and men with the creation of value.

Deere (1976) criticises both Benston and Dalla Costa for depicting household production as part of a *pre*-capitalist production unit: 'The household, as the domestic unit of the bourgeois family, was created by the development of capitalism, as social production within the family unit was divorced from the production and reproduction of labour power' (Deere, 1976:17). The family is not an ahistorical, universal institution. It was not 'taken over' by capitalism nor 'subordinated to' it; the family's relation to capital has been a changing one. Patriarchy as an ideology was subordinated to the needs of capital and hence we have the patriarchal family. But even this family type is not a static or a singular one, as it changes in response to external factors and varies according to the class within which it is located. Domestic labour also changes in relation to capital, as we shall see.

The sexual division of labour was regarded as something which could be abolished on a *technical* level. Harrison, for instance, was concerned only with the 'tangible' aspects of domestic work. The ideological role of the family and its contribution to capital is not recognised in his analysis. It was only later, with the integration of psychoanalytic theory and theories of ideology, that the sexual division of labour was recognised as being constituted at a more fundamental level than at the technical one.

The importance attached to women as housewives assumes that women are to a large extent confined within the domestic sphere, which then forms the basis of their oppression (or exploitation, depending on the theory). This is *empirically* the case while women are primarily responsible for domestic work, although this does not account sufficiently for the work they do in the paid labour force. To build theories around this empirical fact—in terms of the contribution of domestic labour to capital—is to mistake the work for the people who are doing it. Again, to use Harrison as an example, if men and women shared this work, what would become of his argument? Housework would either become a matter for the working-class movement, or it would lose all political relevance. In the argument presented by Campioni and her associates the oppression of bourgeois women is not dealt with adequately. If its basis were not economic but simply ideological, it could, on their thesis, be overcome independently, giving bourgeois women no reason to make common cause with their proletarian sisters. It is a naive moral voluntarism to suggest that they should give up the interests they have as part of the capitalist class. As we shall see, when the problem is reformulated and housework is defined in relation to the individual consumption of the wage labourer, the political implications for the working-class movement begin to emerge.

In economic terms, the focus needs to be on the nature of the work, whereas in these theories the concentration has been on the fact that women do it. Once the relationship of the work to capital is understood, then the effects of patriarchal ideology can be determined. This spans all classes and has different effects on each at different moments in history. The theories referred to so far either attribute a determining role to patriarchal ideology in allocating women to a structural group, or the women–domestic work connection is seen as the determining factor.

Domestic labour and capitalist production

During this period an attempt was made to define women in terms of the ahistorical categories of productive and unproductive labour rather than looking at the changed relationship of housework to paid work under varying conditions.

Two major exceptions to this theme were published before the end of 1975 by Seccombe (1974) and Gardiner (1975). Both these authors restricted their analyses to the working class and both attempted an historical account of the changes that have occurred to women and their work within the family.

Feminist commentators on the work of people such as Harrison and Seccombe attributed a great deal of importance to the fact that Marxists outside the women's movement were attempting to apply Marxist concepts and theory to domestic labour. Hence they spent a great deal of time on their contributions:

> One aspect of Seccombe's article that is to be welcomed is that it reflects a growing recognition by Marxists outside the women's liberation movement of the need to consider the productive aspect of women's role in the family and the economic and not just ideological function of the proletarian family in capitalist society. (Gardiner, 1975:48)

Many articles combined a critique of these people with a development of the authors' own ideas (see Gardiner, 1975; Coulson et al., 1975).

To recognise the economic significance of domestic labour it is not necessary either to argue that it is productive in the same sense as wage-labour producing surplus value or to postulate a separate mode of production. Without adopting either position, Seccombe develops an analysis of domestic labour and its contribution to the creation of value which foreshadows in some respects the issues raised in later discussions. At the time of publication, his contributions were assessed in the context of the rather narrow current preoccupation with the distinction between productive and unproductive labour, with the result that the full significance of his work went unacknowledged. He made it clear that '[s]ince the purpose here is to situate the housewife as a labourer I shall concentrate almost entirely on the *production side* of her relation to capital' (1974:5, my emphasis).

By restricting himself to the domestic labour done within working-class families, he avoids the argument that women form a class different from that of categories of men. He discusses the role that domestic labour within working-class families plays in the creation of value. He sees domestic labour's unique character in this fact: '[It] contributes directly to the creation of the commodity labour power while having no direct relation with capital. It is this special *duality* which defines the character of domestic labour under capitalism' (1974:9).

Seccombe rejects Dalla Costa's argument that the housewife is a productive worker and that surplus value is extracted from her labour. He suggests that domestic labour is unproductive and conforms with Marx's description of unproductive labour, 'exchanged not with capital but with revenue, that is, wages or profits' (1974:11). He asks whether categorising domestic work as unproductive negates the assertion that it creates value, and answers that it does not. The law of value does not govern domestic labour, as it is privatised and removed from the arena of the appropriation of surplus value. But this work nevertheless creates and transfers value. This makes domestic labour 'an integral (though separated) part of the totality of capitalist production relations' (n.d.:29). The significance which he attaches to this is explained thus:

> Seeing the common interests of all those who create value, understanding the necessity of their common activity to a common (anti-capitalist) end ... this is working-class consciousness. While people arrive at this understanding in different ways, the point is that the theory of value and political class consciousness are complementary components of an integrated whole. (n.d.:30)

So the analysis is geared to the objective position of the working-class housewife, and the impact of her position and function on her consciousness (1974:19).

Seccombe, stressing the absence of a direct relation between capital and domestic labour, argues against Dalla Costa here, pointing to the objective limitations to the capacity of women as housewives for political struggle: 'Mass abstention from the house-hold is simply not an option for working-class housewives. Dalla Costa and James consistently ignore the economic compulsion of work under capitalism both in the home and in the factory' (1974:22).

Critics of Seccombe miss the point that he makes about the 'economic functions' of the housewife's work. Seccombe did not confine himself to the production of use-values (cleaning, cooking, etc.), but referred, as did Dalla Costa, to the 'intangible' aspects of the economic functions of domestic labour. This is clearly set out in his article, where he conceptually distinguishes the 'economic' and the 'ideological' functions. Within the first he itemises not only the physical maintenance of the worker, but the psychological maintenance and the socialisation of children in terms of required skills, and so on, that are involved in this work each day and through the generations. His was a partial analysis,[9] and in a second article, responding to his critics, he makes his position clearer.

In his first paper, Seccombe focused on domestic labour's relation to paid labour, and assumed full-time domestic labour for the purposes of his analysis. In his second paper, he accepted the criticism of Coulson and her associates (1975) that, while analysing the relation of housework to paid work generally, his 'political conclusions were over-extended . . . given the absence of a second level of analysis specifying *domestic labour's relation to women's wage labour in particular*' (Coulson et al., 1975:85).

To illustrate his case, Seccombe uses the example of the effects on domestic labour when the price of labour-power falls below its value. When this occurs, does it show up in a lowered standard of living for the working-class? Seccombe answers that it does not. It is managed in one of two ways: through the intensification of domestic labour, or through the wife taking paid employment. These are the two alternatives which he sees as open to the working-class family. The wife, by taking employment, offers capital what it constantly seeks—an expansion of surplus labour time from the same population. When the wife goes out to work, household costs increase. Her wage fills the gap between the old single wage and the new expanded cost of reproducing the family's labour-power (n.d.:29).

Contrary to most theorists at the time, Seccombe had pointed out that there may be a limit on the industrialisation, or socialisation of domestic labour under capitalism: 'As long as capitalism exists, so will a residual core of private domestic labour. For how else could a class of free labourers, deprived of surplus and ownership in the means of production, reproduce itself from one day to the next, much less from one generation to the next?' (1975:96).

Gardiner (1975) combines a critique of Seccombe with the development of her own ideas. She argues that domestic labour does not create value as Seccombe suggests, but that it contributes to surplus value by keeping down necessary labour, or the value of labour-power, to a level that is lower than the actual subsistence level of the working-class. Gardiner situates her analysis historically so that she can explain the extent to which services in the home became industrialised at certain points in relation to capital's needs for either women's paid labour or the expansion of markets for commodities. She also indicates the role domestic labour plays in times of crisis when women are forced to work harder in the home to stretch the reduced wages coming in: 'It is interesting to note, for example, that in 1971, a year of very high unemployment and acceleration in the rise of food prices, convenience food sales fell by 5 per cent whilst seasonal food sales rose by 4 per cent, a dual reversal of long-term trends up to that point' (1975:57).

Gardiner avoids the argument about whether the housewife is productive or unproductive, but nevertheless explains housework in relation to the creation of surplus value for capital. In a later article, written with Himmelweit and Mackintosh (1975), there is a significant shift in the argument. They concentrate, as Seccombe did, on the relationship between women's paid and unpaid work: 'such an analysis is the specific contribution of political economy to the women's movement'. They begin by setting out a theoretical problem: the relation of domestic labour to the process by which surplus value is generated within capitalism. At an abstract level they decide that the work of the housewife should be disconnected from the labour theory of value. Domestic work does not contribute to surplus value: 'So the relation of domestic labour to the production of surplus value, is simply that the former makes the latter possible' (Gardiner et al., 1975:13).

ˑ They argue that any account of the relationship of domestic labour to capital must be historically situated. The connection is made between domestic work and the reproduction of the capitalist system as a totality (1975:13). This draws attention not only to the relation between women's paid and unpaid work, but to the relation of women's and men's paid labour and the variable connection between domestic work and the booms and recessions of capitalism. They have pointed to some of the areas which need further empirical investigation. However, until this was carried out, some unexamined assumptions remained and in this paper there are three which must be questioned. The first is that the existence of full-time domestic labour within the working class is an indication that 'capital has been unable to overcome the obstacles to complete socialisation of domestic labour' (1975:13); secondly, that labour-saving technology releases women from the home to participate in paid labour, and that, indeed, this participation is *conditioned* to a large extent by the introduction of labour-saving devices into the home. A commonly held assumption is that labour-saving devices have 'decreased the amount of socially necessary labour that goes into domestic duties, thereby releasing the woman for recruitment into the cheap labour force' (Campioni et al., 1974b:12; see also Coulson et al., 1975:67).

The argument that the socialisation of domestic work, to the extent that this process has occurred, is a 'process of freeing women for wage labour' has limited application. Since the advent of capitalism women have always worked as wage labourers. Labour-saving devices have only been generally available to the Western working class in the last two decades. Even now 'basic' items such as washing machines and refrigerators are by no means in every home.[10] The effects of domestic labour-saving technology in different segments of the working class are not clear, but it is certain that at various times and in different sections of the working class, women have performed both paid and unpaid work without much in the way of labour-saving devices, simply spending longer hours at their work.

More generally, though, while the authors point to the historically specific nature of the connection between domestic labour and capital, they are left with a static and invariable conception of the relation between patriarchal ideology and the class structure. Gardiner and her co-authors (1975:7) make it clear that, as far as the 'relations of domestic labour' are concerned, husbands benefit from the work of their wives. However, this relationship within the family is not explored between classes, nor in terms of its variation in response to wider economic and social changes. While women's unpaid labour is seen economically to be of benefit to capital, and psychologically to be of benefit to males, they are unable to specify historically the connection between patriarchal ideology and the class structure.

Women, domestic labour and legitimation

I shall use two articles to illustrate the application of these theoretical developments to the history of women's paid and unpaid work in the United States. This type of investigation is also under way in Australia and in Britain.[11]

Milkman, in 'Women's work and economic crises: some lessons of the Great Depression' (1976), traces women's work experiences through the Great Depression as well as during the period following World War II, and then considers how the situation of women in the 1970s compares with their situation during the crisis of the 1930s. The paper modifies an idea taken for granted in the theories considered so far: that women form a homogeneous group of potential labour which can be shuttled in and out of the workforce according to the needs of capital. Milkman contests this assumption that women can be drawn on in periods when labour is scarce and expelled in periods of labour surplus. She sees that this can be neither a sufficient nor valid explanation of the cultural definition of women as primarily wives and mothers, nor of their lack of class consciousness as workers (1976:74).

While it is true that in periods of economic expansion women tend to enter the paid workforce, Milkman points out that the postwar boom period is the usual single example of the whole thesis of women forming a reserve labour force. She indicates that in periods of recession the situation is more complicated. The complexity is partly explained by the 'consistent pattern of labour market segmentation by sex' (Milkman, 1976:76). The female sector of the labour market includes jobs of a type which do not attract men, as they are closely bound up with cultural definitions of what is appropriate for women to do. The jobs at issue are regarded as extensions of the sort of work that women perform within the home or are symbolically equivalent, in terms of the relationships involved. For example, much clerical and secretarial work is done in subordinate and supportive relations to male workers.

This means that the contradiction between the cultural definition of women as primarily mothers and wives, and their definition as 'workers', is not sharp. The predicted effects, then, of women participating in paid labour—the breaking up of the family unit, the increased awareness of women, both of their oppression and of their class consciousness—have not occurred. Milkman suggests, in fact, that women's involvement in paid work during the depression of the 1930s had a contrary effect: that the sex-typing of jobs served to blunt women's consciousness of themselves as workers. Further, the effect on family life was contrary to the usual supposition:[12]

> To say that the unemployed father lost status in the family would seem to imply that women who assumed the role of

> 'provider' gained somehow. But such a role reversal was not
> a simple exchange of power . . . If there was any increased
> recognition of woman's economic role in the family, it did
> not represent a gain in status, for no one was comfortable
> with the new state of affairs, and the reversal of roles was
> resented by everyone involved. (1976:83)

During times of economic contraction women are not necessarily the
first to lose employment. Even during the 1930s the segmentation of jobs
did not allow much movement of males into the female sector. The combined effects of this segmentation with the already existing relationships
within the family meant that 'women workers' in employment continued
to be distinguished from 'workers':

> This helps to mediate the contradiction between the continu-
> ing need for women's unpaid work in the family and the
> tendency for women's work to be increasingly integrated
> into the sphere of paid production for profit. Sex-typing is
> an ideological mechanism which denies the existence of any
> conflict between women's family role and their role in paid
> labour, blithely labelling both as 'women's work'. (Milkman,
> 1976:78)

Milkman's thesis forces a modification of some assumptions previously held. Women were not and generally are not competing directly
for men's jobs, although this is how popular opinion and the media, as
well as some of the trade unions, represent the matter. The attitude of
the trade unions reflects not so much collusion with capital[13] as a generalised expression of what many male workers feel—that while women
have jobs and there is a high unemployment rate, men's position in the
family is undermined, resting as it does on their being the main or sole
income providers. The 'reserve army' thesis requires modification to the
extent that the employment and unemployment of males and females are
in some degree independent of each other, though the thesis may be more
applicable to times of recession than Milkman allows.

In an article pursuing the same theme, 'Women: scapegoats and safety
valves in the Great Depression' (1976), Humphries points to the possibility that, rather than one sex taking the jobs of the other, there can occur
downward mobility within both male and female sectors, with resulting
high unemployment at lower levels. Within the female sector, those who
lose employment in 'higher-status' jobs are likely to take the jobs that are
less affected by unemployment, but are needed more, in economic terms,
by the women who are currently filling them (see Power, 1978, for a similar pattern in Australia). So, not only is a division set up between the

sexes within the working class, but between ethnic groups and races within the female sector as well. It is possible, too, that those who are in the 'higher-status' jobs are the women whose husbands could afford to maintain them as full-time domestic workers, which would not be the case in the lower parts of the occupational structure.

If some jobs are distinctly 'women's jobs' or 'men's jobs', others are not. Both men and women are teachers and para-medical workers, for instance. In these fields, however, there is a sexual hierarchy. Men take the jobs with higher status, salary and authority, women the lower. This situation indicates the need for a further modification of the thesis as Milkman presents it. In some of these jobs there is an incursion of males into what have previously been regarded as female occupational categories (social work, primary teaching, nursing). A contradiction for the feminist movement during times of high unemployment is highlighted in these cases. For example, feminists have argued for the importance of having male teachers at the preschool and infants levels. This is increasingly occurring, but at the expense of female employment.

The particular value of Humphries' research is that it points to the *legitimating* aspect of the relationship between women's experiences of paid and unpaid labour:

> [C]apitalists individually, the owning class collectively, and institutions representative of such groups, have a dual interest. They are interested in the continued expansion of capital and increasing commodity production associated with the search for profits, but this requires the perpetuation of the capitalist system and the power relationships inherent in that system. (Humphries, 1976:99)

Humphries suggests that the effects of women's 'socialisation into feminine gender identity' indicates that 'patriarchal relations are suspiciously convenient for capitalism' (1976:100). She refers to the ways in which institutions such as the family, the education system and the workplace have a legitimating role for capitalism, having a part to play in the reproduction of the class structure. Capitalism is not simply a goods-producing and capital-accumulating system: 'A great amount of labour time in capitalist society is spent in activities that have the purpose of perpetuating capitalist relations of production, rather than producing necessary goods' (Zaretsky, 1976:70).

Humphries' work on the depression of the 1930s stresses the social-control aspects of the processes to which Milkman refers. Having pointed to the dual needs of capital she argues that these might conflict at particular times and that such conflicts may be mediated through the intervention of ideological processes. For instance, women's paid work during periods of recession may reinforce rather than challenge the traditional allocation of behaviour appropriate to the sexes.

During the depression women were urged to stay out of the paid work-force and encouraged to stay at home because there they would consume more and thus hasten economic recovery. Humphries gives examples of how this tactic was used (1976:111–12). Research at the time indicated that marriage, the formation of new households and traditional family patterns have a positive effect on the demand for an important range of products in the area of consumer durables: 'Homemaking still ranked first as the occupation employing the largest number of persons, expending the longest hours in labour, and *possessing the largest purchasing power*' (Humphries, 1976:111). Humphries argues that 'In a depression, as at no other time, does industry need women as *consumers* rather than as *producers*' (1976:113). However, this does not indicate how particular families might respond to this need. It is a common assumption that full-time housewives necessarily consume more. Feminist literature provides few exceptions. A typical description is given by Rubinstein:

> 'The privatised nature of housework also benefits capitalism by providing a market for an ever-increasing range of con-sumer goods. Women alone, with only a television or radio for company, are the ideal audience for saturation advertis-ing, playing on their insecurities, and convincing them that love and admiration will be theirs with X brand detergent, make-up or instant soup. (1976:10)

Humphries indicates that not all classes of women were affected in the same way, but she argues that the consumption standards of 'middle-class' women drove working-class women out to work so that they could afford the consumer items that they were encouraged to buy: '[T]hus in emulating their better-off sisters working-class women helped out on the consumption front and paid for this privilege with wage labour' (1976:114).

These arguments are functionalist in tone, relying as they do on the requirements of industry with the associated assumption of women being passive recipients of the advertising propaganda directed at them. Such an assumption cannot apply to those women with no power to stretch the wage other than by the intensification and duration of domestic work. The consumption patterns of some working-class women who were in paid employment could hardly have been an imitation of their 'middle-class sisters' because many could not have afforded to do this. It is likely that for some, consumer items purchased were services and other replacements for domestic labour. It is likely that in some segments of the working class women worked in order to maintain present or past standards of living, and that the 'consumer durables' remained beyond their means.

There are areas here that need empirical investigation: what the consumption patterns are in households where women are full-time domestic workers and where they are not, and how this varies at different income levels as well as how the choices are arrived at in relation to perceived needs.

Further, the idea that *full*-time housewives at all levels of the wage structure consume more consumer durables must be examined more critically. This might apply to women whose husbands are on higher wages, but in the lower segments of the workforce wives in paid employment may consume more services, and if they are at home full-time they are unlikely to be able to afford the consumer durables that are available. Humphries indicates that it was 'middle-class' women whose husbands could afford full-time housewives and that these were also the group that could reinvigorate consumer spending. So the value of these women as consumers was important, but this cannot be generalised across classes. The anti-feminist ideology which promoted traditional family patterns at the end of the depression reinforced the way of life of 'middle-class' women, but Milkman speculates that this induced feelings of guilt and resentment in the working-class wives.

Brennan, in 'Women and work' (1977), applies these theoretical developments to the situation of migrant women in the workforce in Australia. She sets out to explain the historical significance of full-time domestic labour, not to capital, but to the working class. She criticises earlier writing for its failure to account adequately for the existence of full-time housework: 'Overall, the attempt to use value theory to explain full-time domestic labour in terms of its *functions* for capital has failed' (Brennan, 1977:40).

Brennan takes as her points of departure two main propositions: (Adamson et al., 1976): first, that domestic work does not produce value or surplus value, and second, that there has to be a period outside the working day when domestic tasks are performed by the working class. She adds to these points insights drawn from analyses of the ways in which the labour market is segmented along sex, ethnic and racial lines. Brennan describes the pattern in Australia:

> Currently, it appears that there are six broad segments in
> the Australian labour market, hierarchically ranked as fol-

lows: males born in Australia, Britain and Ireland, as well as
those born in Northern Europe, the United States, Canada
and New Zealand; southern European males, including those
born in Turkey and Yugoslavia; black males; and then the
three corresponding groups of women workers. (1977:43)

Brennan dismisses the view that full-time domestic labour might have
any direct economic benefits to capital. She points to the ways in which
housework by working-class women, when performed full-time, involves
a *loss* for capital. She does this by following Marx's enunciation of the
ways in which surplus value extraction is increased or decreased, depending on the relative size of the population involved and the historically
determined value of labour-power. The existence of full-time housewives
within the working class implies that the wage of a labourer is a family
wage, and the loss for capital occurs in the following ways:

The production of use-values in the home cuts expenditure
outside it, which at least raises the possibility that the
family's living standard could be raised above that implied
by the value of labour-power ... More definitively, the
family wage means that the working class has *some* control
of the labour supply: if less working class people are needed
to work, then competition for jobs is less, and therefore the
price of labour-power is higher. (Brennan, 1977:41)

Brennan looks at the significance of full-time housework for the working
class by tracing it historically, and indicates that progressive erosion of
the concept of the family wage in Australia has been of general benefit to
capital. When there is more than one wage coming into the same family,
more surplus value is extracted, considering that, previously, the value of
labour-power was based on the subsistence needs of a wage labourer and
his dependants. The notion of a family wage only applies at the upper
levels of the wage structure in Australia at the present time.

At the lower levels of the wage structure, it is necessary to have more
than one income in a family to maintain a reasonable standard of living.
Capital benefits not only in the way indicated above, but in terms of the
increased consumption of services and commodities, as domestic labour
is to some extent replaced by the purchase of ready-made articles. The
data Brennan draws upon tend to show that some segments of the working class need to respond with more than one strategy in order to maintain their standard of living, combining wage labour with an intensification of domestic work (see also Milkman, 1976).

It is clear from this research that the women who have to take jobs are most likely to be married to men in the lower segments of the labour market. Full-time domestic labour is no longer a 'gain' for the working class at the lower levels because these families can no longer afford to live on one wage. However, if full-time domestic work at the upper levels of the wage structure is carried on at the expense of the lower levels—since people there can only maintain their standard of living by relying on more than one income—this is not a gain to the working class as a whole: 'The family wage once implied benefit for the whole working-class, but this no longer holds. While the upper segments of the labour market may still earn an effective family wage, the basis for a family wage for all working-class males has been undermined' (Brennan, 1977:48).

However, there is a serious flaw in this argument. I have indicated above that most working-class families have in recent years depended on *more than one income* to maintain their standard of living. Brennan, and those who preceded her, assume that this involves the employment of women, but there are clearly other possibilities. This is a most significant qualification. Consider the influence of the ideology of the male-as-breadwinner. Domestic labour continues to be done full-time in many families where there is more than one income. Either the husband works two jobs, or works overtime, or another member of the family (or household) earns, while the wife–mother stays at home.

In fact, there is evidence to suggest that this is widespread.[14] All the contributions to this discussion fail to consider, let alone explain, the fact that many women, in families for which the wage is not a family wage, do not seek employment. There are several possible alternatives. There may be an increase in the use of social services, although this is a diminishing option under governmental cutbacks. Families may reduce their standard of living and there seems no doubt that this is a course followed by some. There may be an intensification of domestic labour coupled with a reliance on relatives or part-time work, perhaps performed in the home—taking in washing, ironing, looking after people's children and so on. The other, already mentioned, is that the husband or some other member of the family may take on two jobs or work overtime.

Which option is taken depends on a great many things, including the relative unemployment rates for the male and female segments of the labour market, and the attitudes people hold to the question of family responsibilities. As Humphries points out,

> economic circumstances impinge on this decision through a complex set of social pressures. Households' preferences for income or leisure, or more accurately for home produced

goods or purchased goods, are critically sensitive to the
social environment and specifically to prevailing attitudes to
women, married women working, the value of home life and
so on. (1976:110)

An explanation further to Brennan's, for the existence of full-time
domestic labour at these lower levels of the wage structure, then needs to
be introduced: the ways in which women's paid and unpaid labour are
connected does not sufficiently account for women's subordination. As
Brennan says, the other writers do not fully explain full-time domestic
labour. Brennan explains this in relation to her view of the family wage
as a gain to the working class which has been undermined. But this does
not explain full-time domestic labour either, to the extent that it persists
at lower levels of the wage structure. Further illumination of this pattern
can be gained by an analysis of patriarchal ideology.

Conclusions

To effect change, people need to know what systematic variations there
are within each sex and class. Other theoretical perspectives become
important here. In Australia many of the theorists who concerned themselves initially with the 'domestic labour debate' have since moved on to
deal with theories of ideology and psychoanalysis (Brennan, Campioni
and Jacka, 1976; Campioni, 1976b; Jacka, 1977). Whereas previously
the intervention of the ideological was given primacy in determining
women as a structural group (Campioni et al., 1974b), the class structure
is now seen as the main determining factor and attention is given to the
'different expression in different classes' of patriarchal ideology (Campioni, 1976a:1).

In 1976 several papers were delivered at a Political Economy Conference in Australia which together sum up the present state of the argument. At a theoretical level there is on the one hand the argument that
the theory of value has no applicability whatsoever to the status of
domestic labour (Curthoys and Barbalet, 1976). On the other, is Campioni's insistence that it does: '[A]ll labour, which contributes to the production and reproduction of any elements of production has to be considered as part of the process which creates value, in the sense that it is
part of the movement of total social capital—that is, the process of capitalist accumulation' (1976a:2).

Campioni is going back, in a reformulated way, to her original assertion that the 'intangible' aspects of women's work are important in repro-

ducing the relations of domination and subordination which exist in the wider capitalist society. So a shift has occurred, with the emphasis now on the '*patriarchal* family, while at the same time avoiding the blurring of class differences' (Campioni, 1976a:1).

To restrict the work of the housewife to the 'individual consumption of the wage labourer' (Curthoys and Barbalet, 1976) is to ignore other important aspects of the work, most notably the reproduction of the social relations of capitalist production. This reproduction includes not merely the physical process involved with the fitness and skills of labourers. Attitudes, personality formation and the internalisation of relations of domination and subordination are part of the same labour process—the work that women perform in the home. Given this, one must question whether it is valid, even as an analytic distinction, to separate the economic and ideological dimensions of domestic work.

Similarly, women's domestic work cannot be understood only from the point of view of capital accumulation. The early claims by radical feminists, that women's domestic labour was of benefit to all males, has more recently been given more sophisticated treatment, and not in isolation from the analysis of the patterning of women's paid labour. 'Women's unpaid domestic labour advantages not only their husbands, but supports the whole structure of wages and profits in the labour market and subsidises public expenditure in the state sector' (Baldock and Cass, 1983:xii). We must not lose sight of the fact, too, that worker organisations have contributed to the structuring of the labour market along sex and other lines. Both Hartmann (1976) and Rubery (1980) have developed this perspective in ways that I would like briefly to address.

Hartmann points to the trade union response to claims that worker activity has exacerbated the problems of women's employment opportunities, a response which draws attention to the material benefits the union movement has achieved overall, thereby drawing attention away from the subjective and material benefits male workers are attempting to maintain, both within the labour market and within the family. Rubery places less stress on the benefits to individual males within the family and at work, and is more concerned with what collectively the trade union movement has traded off in relation to benefits historically gained. She quite correctly criticises theories which overstress 'the control offered by the bureaucratic division of the labour force, and at the same time underestimat[e] or ignor[e] the benefits for the working class of a sheltered, secure, albeit stratified, labour market' (1980:266). She suggests that a bargaining position may only be established and maintained through the development of a structured labour force and that the methods used offer varying degrees of control for management. The difference between this approach and Hartmann's is that Rubery's is a more dispassionate glance—looking at the total context and demonstrating that trade union activity is not, on the whole, benefiting women.

So, it is incorrect to say, as Brennan does, that labour market segmentation results only from capital's seeking out the cheapest possible labour-power to perform a certain task. This segmentation serves many purposes and may not be in the immediate and direct interests of capital. Women's paid and unpaid work need to be analysed in relation to historical shifts and variations in patriarchal ideology and how this informs the ways in which the capitalist system as a whole is reproduced. Organisational, as against occupational, analysis is being developed in order to draw attention to actual practices within firms and industries, managerial control techniques and worker responses to changes in the labour process. (See West, 1982; Burton, 1983; Cockburn, 1983; Game and Pringle, 1983.) This type of analysis enables concrete demonstrations to be made of the political and legitimising aspects of capitalist social relations as they operate within the labour process. In other words, a reconceptualisation of the issue of the relationship between women's paid and unpaid work draws attention to the active agency of both worker organisations and managerial processes, rather than simply identifying management's agency in the interests of capital.

What remains in question, after all this argument, is whether the labour theory of value has any application to domestic work. I would suggest that it does, but not in the static way in which it has been analysed so far. It is as a process over time that the connection of domestic labour to the extraction of surplus value can be understood, and the process is an uneven one, depending on the success of working-class demands, relative unemployment levels and the possibilities there are for the intensification of domestic work. What has not been considered enough are the limits to this: for instance, mending and 'cooking from scratch' and so on, are options available. But other costs—for instance, those of education and medical expenses—mean that, regardless of the intensification of domestic work, under conditions of recession the living standards of the working class may be lowered.

The relationship between the labour theory of value and domestic work could be summarised in this way: there are different ways in which the extraction of surplus value can be increased. The one way which is relevant to domestic work is where wages are below the value of labour-power, while this is defined in terms of a wage labourer and his or her dependants at a historically specified level of subsistence. To this situation, working-class responses may be: first, the intensification of domestic labour, with its inherent limits; second, a lowering of the living standards of the working class, also historically with its own limits; third, the wife–mother taking employment; and fourth, the husband–father or others in the family/household apart from the wife–mother taking on overtime or more than one job, leaving a full-time domestic labourer in the home.

The last two are of interest to capital in a strict economic sense, involving the extraction of surplus value from the same labouring population. The ways in which the working class deals with its 'individual consumption' are of no direct interest to capital. The first two are relevant to capital to the extent that they may result in pressures from the working class—for increased wages and a decrease in working hours, through which mechanisms the labour theory of value comes into play once more.

None of the theories, so far, deal with the fourth point above. With Brennan's work, we can see three possible reasons why. First, she deals only with women in the paid workforce. Second, she separates the 'political economy' aspect from the ideological intervention of patriarchal relationships. Third, she focuses on the abstract demands of capital at the expense of a range of strategies which come to bear in the labour market with effects on women's domestic labour.

Theories of labour-market segmentation and other approaches used to explain the relation between women's paid and unpaid labour are inadequate while the relationship is seen only in terms of capital accumulation at any particular point in time. Although this might be a necessary perspective for a long-term understanding, it undervalues the fruitfulness of a perspective which stresses the strategic actions of different parties in the creation of 'segments and shelters' (Freedman, 1976) in the labour market. The perspective which gives a central place to male worker organisations' protectionist strategies designed to protect a position in the labour market and in the home points to their influence on ideologies of women's place. These ideologies partly create and sustain circumstances by which women's strategic planning in relation to taking up new opportunities in the labour market are undermined. Some policy implications of the conclusions reached using such a perspective will be discussed in the final chapter.

The complex and contradictory connections between institutional arrangements, such as the family, the school, the state and the labour market, are important to a further understanding of 'the tenacity of sexual asymmetry and inequality' (Chodorow, 1978:6). Some of these connections will be examined in the following two chapters.

5

Psychoanalysis, masculinity/femininity and the family

Socialisation, differentiation, legitimation, labour, are themes which come together in a concept that has been of increasing importance in recent years: that of the reproduction of a system of social relations—or, for short, 'social reproduction'. This chapter deals with the first major attempt to incorporate this theme into feminist thought, which centred on the application of (a reread) psychoanalysis to the reproduction of masculinity and femininity within the family. In the following two chapters I will attempt to show that a number of other bodies of literature, as yet unconnected, can and should be brought into an extended theory of social reproduction.

Freud's work is the basis for this particular theoretical development, but has undergone extensive criticism in the process. The theory of the unconscious is being used in feminist interpretation of the family to produce a more thorough account of the perpetuation not only of women's sense of inferiority, but of male dominance itself. Writers pursuing this line of enquiry have set out to uncover the role of patriarchal ideology in reproducing the social relations of capitalism. They have also been concerned with the way in which patriarchal ideology is itself perpetuated, whether under capitalism or in other modes of production. They have argued that conventional conceptions of socialisation are inadequate.

The notion that children observe parental role-performance, identify with the same-sexed parent and internalise appropriate modes of behaviour as a result of reward and punishment not only fails to account completely for what is to be explained, but imports assumptions about the 'naturalness' of feminine and masculine modes of behaviour and of heterosexuality which are themselves significant elements of patriarchal ideology.

With the acknowledgement of the role of the unconscious, socialisation and the development of the child begin to be seen as more complex
matters. 'Social learning', as usually outlined, must be understood as depending on another process which precedes and accompanies it.

The theory of the unconscious remains an area of active enquiry and
development. All I can do here is point to significant aspects of this
development and perhaps anticipate where it may lead. This means
selecting for attention pieces of work which have been read, discussed,
and written about with particular interest.

Juliet Mitchell and psychoanalysis

There has always been, on the part of the political left, an ambivalent response to psychoanalytic theory—or more particularly perhaps, its practice. This is despite the fact that, since Freud's time, people have tried to
draw together the insights from psychoanalysis and Marxist theory to
understand such things as the authoritarian personality, the relation
between the sexes, the relationship between the class structure of society
and sexuality, and what role the repression of sexuality might play in the
perpetuation of class society or culture/civilisation itself. Reich (1946,
1975) and Marcuse (1972a, 1972b) are examples of these attempts and,
in the context of the 1960s, Reimut Reiche, in *Sexuality and Class
Struggle.* This is also true of the women's movement of the 1960s and
1970s. During this time, further attempts have been made at integration
or reconciliation between Marxism and psychoanalysis. French psycho-
analysts within and outside the women's movement were the first to take
up this task.

As Mitchell points out (1975:xix), the only part of the feminist
movement 'that has been trying consistently for some time to turn
psychoanalytic theory into political practice' was a series of
groups—*Psychanalse et Politique*—which were based in Paris and
constituted a Marxist wing of the feminist movement there. They were
actively denouncing radical feminism's rejection of psychoanalysis and
were using Lacan, critically, for an understanding of the operations of
the unconscious. But it was Juliet Mitchell, in *Psychoanalysis and
Feminism*, who introduced this endeavour to British, American and
Australian audiences (see also Rubin, 1975).

On the whole, before such books as Mitchell's were widely read and
discussed, the attitude towards Freud and his theories from within the
women's movement was a hostile one. As Mitchell says, 'The greater part

of the feminist movement has identified Freud as the enemy' (1975:xiii). Betty Friedan's book, *The Feminine Mystique* (1965), epitomises this attitude. Her discussion of Freud indicates clearly the ways in which psychoanalysis was taken up in America as an 'adaptation' therapy process. This has been commented upon frequently, by Marcuse in *Eros and Civilisation* and by others, including Lacan. It is, one may speculate, the reason why theoretical developments emanating from France were taken up by British Marxists more quickly than they were by American ones. But it was generally the case, within the women's movement until recently, that Freud was accused of reinforcing patriarchal society through his theory and the practice of psychoanalysis.

I have chosen Mitchell's book as a vehicle to explore these ideas because, for the non-French-speaking world, it was her particular attempt to use Freud's theory of the unconscious, in conjunction with Marxism, which has been the focus of discussion within the women's movement, and the book was read widely outside it (see also Zaretsky, 1975). It was specifically (although not explicitly) Althusserian Marxism that she attempted to conjoin with psychoanalysis (Mitchell, 1971). Hence it was mostly Althusserian Marxist-feminists who first responded to Mitchell's ideas and began to examine them critically.

One effect of Mitchell's use of anthropological work, for her analysis of kinship structures in particular, has been to draw the attention of Marxist-feminists to modes of production other than capitalism. It has drawn their attention to the importance not only of anthropological studies generally, but to the work of Marxist anthropologists in particular. There has been, on the whole, a fruitful coming together of what had formerly been seen as two quite distinct areas of study.

In *Psychoanalysis and Feminism* Mitchell was concerned to do two things. She wanted to show feminists that they had thrown out the baby with the bathwater in their rejection of psychoanalysis. At the same time she wanted to point out that a critical appraisal of Freud was required to place his theory of the unconscious in the social context where it developed, in order to eliminate the influence of that context and free it from the contamination of its patriarchal assumptions. She says: 'However it may have been used, psychoanalysis is not a recommendation *for* a patriarchal society, but an analysis *of* one' (Mitchell, 1975:xiii). In fact, she suggests, it should be seen as a theory of patriarchal culture and is therefore invaluable to feminist analysis.

Mitchell's book was written while the debate on domestic labour was, in a sense, drawing to a close, and not very satisfactorily. It is interesting to note, then, that much of the work in the area of psychoanalysis has been carried out by feminists who were also involved in that debate. There was a recognition that the 'psychological' functions attributed to the family or the wife-mother could not adequately be explained without exploration beneath the surface appearances of family life.

There is a confusion in some of the literature in the use of the term 'unconscious'. Freud's concept was integrally bound up with that of repression. Both in theories of socialisation, and in theories of ideology such as that of Althusser 1971 (1978a), unconscious means something else as well—the fact that people do or perceive or accept things as they are, without recognising that they might be, or are, different. The social world as it exists, and the institutions within which we carry out our lives are given, and the extent to which they can be questioned is partly limited by the fact that we know no others. The social world into which we are born has an air of 'naturalness' about it—hence many of our actions, beliefs, and ways of behaving are 'unconscious' in the sense that we take for granted so much and do things and believe things 'unthinkingly'. What appears to be the case is accepted as being the case, and our practices reinforce this attitude towards the world-as-given. I would like to refer to this, provisionally, as 'mis-recognition', a term used by Althusser and others, because it needs to be distinguished from the unconscious of Freud's theory; provisional, because this term also has different meanings. French 'Méconnaissance' is difficult to translate directly. It has been translated as 'failure to recognise', or 'to misrecognise' or 'not knowing'. These words have different meanings in different theoretical frameworks. A more direct translation would be 'bad knowing'.[1] I will be referring to this problem again, at the end of this chapter. But it is important to keep it in mind—this fact of 'mis-recognition' clearly has other implications: for instance, for the methodology of the social sciences. As Eleanor Leacock puts it,

> measurements *ad infinitum* crowd the social science journals only to obscure rather than reveal, and much less prove, anything fundamental about social process. The upshot is to perpetuate the world of social myth in which we perforce live, to measure it, test it, analyse it, 'discover' it—without ever lifting the veil and looking at it! (1972:60)

In terms of a theory of ideology, the relationship between historical materialism and psychoanalysis lies there. It explains the attraction of Marxists to psychoanalysis, as both point to the inadequacy of empiricist positions which take for granted what appears to be the case and test hypotheses in relation to data 'out there' as if they are the only reality, and as if those data are not already theory-laden. The basic point is that one must delve under the surface of things, in order to account for the phenomenal forms which are perceived either by actors in a situation or the observer of those actors or events. The affinity of structural linguistics with these positions is also clear—being concerned with discovering systematic structural relationships which are unknown to the speakers of the language in question.

Psychoanalysis and Feminism is subtitled, 'Freud, Reich, Laing and Women'. But it is Mitchell's treatment of Freud which has chiefly occupied feminist attention. The theory of ideology incorporating the idea of the unconscious derives, of course, from Freud, rather than the other two theorists. Mitchell deals with their work, though judging it 'ultimately unsatisfactory', because she considers that the feminist movement has embraced their radical psychologies in preference to Freud's. Her book is, in part, an attempt to redress this situation.

She presents a searching critique of the theories. Ortner (1975) and Wollheim (1975), in widely read reviews of her book, argue that this is a waste of both Mitchell's and the reader's time, but I disagree. It is necessary to understand the inadequacies of Reich's and Laing's perspectives—to say nothing of those of de Beauvoir, Firestone, Greer, Millett and Figes, with whom she also deals—not only because they have been influential, but because careful examination shows more clearly the importance of the element missing from all of them—the unconscious. Notwithstanding her criticisms, Mitchell is also careful to indicate the value of these various analyses of family life, in different historical circumstances, as contributions to a wider understanding of the ways in which some of the hidden processes work, on the surface of family life.

She cites as an example their attempt to understand the Oedipus complex independently of the unconscious, and comments that this is 'common and fatal'. She believes that both the objections and tributes of Freud's feminist critics are meaningless, because they have attempted to deal with his concept of femininity outside the framework of psychoanalysis. His ideas, she says, are made to sound reactionary in implication chiefly because they are approached without regard to the unconscious. The writers in question deny the unconscious in different ways, 'Reich by finding it to be nothing more than a pool of biological energy, Laing by treating its constructs as though they were identical to those of consciousness, the feminist critics by believing above all in social actuality and conscious choice.' (Mitchell, 1975:356) Mitchell was criticising the reductionism involved in these accounts, in which 'the laws of the primary process (the laws that govern the workings of the unconscious) were replaced by those of the secondary process (conscious

decisions and perceptions)' (Brennan et al., 1976:17-18). The basic theoretical defect is the same, however, and to rectify it is Mitchell's principal
objective.

Mitchell's main contention is that patriarchy has been a universal
feature in all societies; in fact, it is equated with culture itself. While she
acknowledges the generally held disquiet about the vagueness of the
term patriarchy, she uses it in the most general sense. For her, patriarchy means 'the law of the father—and it is the operation of this law
within the life of the individual boy and girl that Freud's work can help
us understand' (1975:xiv). What is interesting here, is that at the time
this book was published, most feminists *did* think that patriarchy had
been a universal feature of human society. The reaction to Mitchell's
book was one of despair and a sense of being appalled: feminists could
not afford to believe that her theory was correct. Notwithstanding
Mitchell's view to the contrary (that the structure of the unconscious, or
its content, can change) this theory made the correspondence between
culture/civilisation and patriarchy absolute. She says:

> It is the specific feature of patriarchy—the law of the hypo-
> thesized pre-historic murdered father—that defines the rela-
> tive places of men and women in human history. This
> 'father' and his representatives—all fathers—are the crucial
> expression of patriarchal society. It is *fathers* not *men* who
> have the determinate power. And it is a question neither of
> biology nor of a specific society, but of *human* society itself.
>
> Such a proposition possibly seems *more* generalized and
> its solution *less* available than the biological-technological
> and sociological theories. But I don't think this need be the
> case. (1975:409)

Mitchell's argument rests on the universality of the process by which
individuals become gendered social subjects, the significant process here
being the Oedipus complex and its resolution. The theory of the unconscious shifts emphasis away from the centrality of the individual's conscious self, and on to the unconscious as constituting the subject. What is
being investigated here is what Althusser so charmingly calls: 'the long
forced march which makes mammiferous larvae into human children,
masculine or *feminine* subjects' (Althusser, 1978c:206).

There are two significant moments of becoming a social being—at the
time of the emergence of the ego during the pre-Oedipal phase, and
during the resolution of the Oedipus complex. Attention is concentrated
here on the Oedipus complex and its resolution, and the laws which
Freud said govern the unconscious process—repression of course, and the

mechanisms of displacement and condensation—the effects of which are discovered, in the process of analysis, in the distorted ways in which unconscious thoughts, wishes, desires emerge at the conscious level through dreams, slips of the tongue, wit, jokes and so on. The Oedipus complex will occupy us particularly as it is the stage in Freud's theory at which the girl and boy take on their feminine and masculine gender identities.

The two laws of condensation and displacement which Freud says govern the unconscious process need to be explained, as when we deal with Lacan we see that it is through these that he brings together language and the unconscious, as he sees these laws as identical to those of metaphor and metonymy, the two laws governing the structure of language.

The term condensation has its roots in psychoanalysis in the way in which a number of dream-thoughts are compressed into one image. Freud says:

> A similarity of any sort between two elements of the unconscious material—a similarity between the things themselves or between their verbal presentations—is taken as an opportunity for creating a third, which is a composite or compromise idea . . . The formation of substitutions and contaminations which occurs in slips of the tongue is accordingly a beginning of the work of condensation which we find taking a most vigorous share in the construction of dreams. (Freud, 1901 (1975):100)

On displacement, he says:[2]

> That product, the dream, has above all to evade the censorship, and with that end in view the dream-work makes use of a *displacement of psychical intensities* to the point of a transvaluation of all psychical values. (1900 (1976):650)

He continues by adding that considerations of representability might involve carrying out fresh displacements. Hence, the essence of dream-thoughts need not be represented in the dream at all. 'The dream is, as it were, *differently centred* from the dream-thoughts—its content has different elements as its central point' (1976:414).

Mitchell correctly points out that it is only through an understanding of the unconscious that the concept of the Oedipus complex can be given any meaning. 'Complex' indicates

> the totality of *repressed unconscious* ideas that surround an emotionally coloured event . . . The Oedipus complex is the

> *repressed* ideas that appertain to the family drama of any
> primary constellation of figures within which the child must
> find its place. It is not the *actual* family situation or the con-
> scious desire it evokes. (Mitchell, 1975:63)

For Mitchell, psychoanalysis is 'about the inheritance and acquisition of
the human order' (1975:401):

> [T]he psychoanalytic concept of the unconscious is a concept
> of mankind's transmission and inheritance of his social (cul-
> tural) laws ... Understanding the laws of the unconscious
> thus amounts to a start in understanding how ideology func-
> tions, how we acquire and live the ideas and laws within
> which we must exist. A primary aspect of the law is that we
> live according to our sexed identity, our ever imperfect 'mas-
> culinity' or 'femininity'. (1975:403)

So, the unconscious that Freud analysed is reformulated: '[it] could thus
be described as the domain of the reproduction of culture or ideology'
(1975:413). To this point, Mitchell's critics have tended to agree. However, they depart when, following Freud and Lacan, she proposes that
the cultural order has been invariably patriarchal, and that since this is
the case, the Oedipus complex is necessarily the process by which the
individual is constructed in terms of gender identity.

Her confidence about the universality of the Oedipus complex and the
associated castration complex, with the resulting inferiorising of women,
derives from her uncritical acceptance of this aspect of Freud's and
Lacan's theories. But it has a lot to do with the way in which she inte-
grates Lévi-Strauss into her account. She relies on his two related ideas
of the incest taboo and the exchange of women by men. Since Mitchell
fuses them considerably, it is useful to clarify the differences between
Lévi-Strauss and Freud, in relation both to the incest taboo and to the
unconscious.

Freud and Lévi-Strauss differed on the origin and perpetuation of the
incest taboo. Lévi-Strauss (1969) was critical of Freud's historical reconstruction of this and argues that it is not a repressed guilt taboo and does
not arise from incestuous desire. Lévi-Strauss does not argue for incest
being a preferred sexual relation, as it is for Freud in relation, first, to
the mother, but a sexual relation which had to be prohibited for the
inauguration of society. It is part of neither nature (i.e. natural) nor culture (i.e. an invention) but, precisely, both: on the boundary between
them.[3] The incest taboo can only arise with society, and society can only
exist when the family enters into relationships with other families. This,

in Lévi-Strauss's theory, is through the exchange of women by men, and the mother's brother plays the central role, being the mediator between families.

As far as the unconscious is a shared concept, Mitchell's use of it involves a slippery juxtaposition of Freud's and Lévi-Strauss's ideas. They differ radically, unless one places more emphasis on the arguments Freud presents when considering the phylogenetic bases for the content of the unconscious mind. But differences remain even here. The Lévi-Straussian notion that the structure of the unconscious mind imposes structure on external reality in such a way that there is a structural sameness, a correspondence between the form of thought and the form of society (Lévi-Strauss, 1963:79–80), has little to do with Freud's theory of the unconscious. Further, Freud proposes that the unconscious comes into being at the moment of primary repression: that it is not 'there' from birth.

So Mitchell's use of Lévi-Strauss here—and, one might add, her use of him is given force by Lacan's approval of the emphasis placed on the mother's brother as the personification of the symbolic father—is partly clarifying, and partly misses the point. She stresses that one does not need the nuclear family to produce the Oedipus complex. She moves away from the empiricist position that bases the Oedipal trauma on the observations of children and the threats of parents. The father does not have to be present for the drama to be played out: the law of the father operates in his absence. But she nevertheless emphasises the importance of the mother's brother as a visible presence, as a real and powerful representative of this symbolic order. She says: 'In order to establish the socio-cultural break with the circularity of the biological given of two parents and their child, a fourth term must intervene. This is where the mother's brother comes in with the very inauguration of society, he is essential to it' (Mitchell, 1975:375). Mitchell's analysis relies on the bringing together of Lévi-Strauss's universality of the exchange of women and the incest prohibition, and, following Freud and Lacan, the universality of the Oedipus complex, through an acceptance of the law of the father.

Mitchell's position, then, is that one can assert the 'eternal' nature of the unconscious and that the basic structure of the unconscious can be said to be 'universal'—the law of the father is the determining factor for society itself. 'Eternal' is a useful term here, as 'universal' can mean different things—statistical universality, that is, empirically-always universal, or theoretical universality in the sense of conceptual tools. An analogous 'eternal' would be the fact of biological reproduction. This is an important distinction to make when dealing with Mitchell or others who believe that while patriarchy has been empirically universal, it does not have to be—that is, it is not an eternal phenomenon.

Mitchell concludes that women's situation can only be understood through analysis of kinship structures, that even in industrial societies, where the significance of kinship structures might be obscure, it is in this domain that the women's struggle must be waged. In other words, the class struggle is separately situated in capitalist economic arrangements, and the subordination of women is connected to the transhistorical fact of men exchanging women through the kinship system. She argues that patriarchy describes the universal culture, but that in capitalist society this is no longer necessary. This means, then, that the *content* of the unconscious can now change:

> When the potentialities of the complexities of capital-
> ism—both economic and ideological—are released by its over-
> throw, new structures will gradually come to be represented
> in the unconscious. It is the task of feminism to insist on
> their birth. Some other expression of the entry into culture
> than the implication for the unconscious of the exchange of
> women will have to be found in non-patriarchal society. (Mit-
> chell, 1975:415)

What we need is a kinship analysis of contemporary capitalist society, for it is within kinship structures that women, as women, are situated (Mitchell, 1975:370).

Mitchell purports to be analysing sexual/social relations and sexuality as a way of organising society. She gives the example of China to make her point. A visitor to Chinese communes asked, why were the women not in the same, equivalent powerful political positions as the men? And what did the few powerful women have in common? Mitchell says this latter is a feminist question and (therefore) gets a new answer. The Chinese principle was that communes were organised around kinship groups—they had eliminated all that they had seen as exploitative and oppressive in the old system. But by keeping the communes as kinship structures they had retained the exchange of women. Women always moved out of the commune of their origin and married into the new commune of their husband. Mitchell claims that the process in our own society is similar for women where they move out of the families into which they are born. This is symbolically expressed through the taking on of the names of their husbands. In the Chinese communes, the only women who had power positions which were equivalent to men were the ones who married newcomers to their communes. Mitchell says: 'sexual

relationships or kinship relationships are a social principle of organisation and psychoanalysis is about the internalising of those kinship laws
and it is therefore about social relationships' (Mitchell and Zaretsky,
1974).

In arguing this, she separates patriarchy out as a universal, ideological manifestation not confined to specific modes of production. This
leads her to argue that feminist struggle is separate from the working-
class struggle against capitalist relations of exploitation. So the question
becomes, for her: 'how adequately does psychoanalysis analyse ideology
and sexuality, and if it does so, what is the political practice which follows from this theory?' (1975:xx). She then goes on to say—and this is
where much of the criticism is levelled at her—'It may be true to assert
that the women's struggle is determinately against patriarchal ideology
where the class struggle is against bourgeois economic power, but
although both struggles have to take place on the political level, the two
situations do not have parity'.

Althusser and many of Mitchell's critics argue that 'no theory of
psychoanalysis can be produced without basing it on historical materialism (*on which the theory of the formation of familial ideology
depends, in the last instance*)' (Althusser, 1978c:190). Mitchell, on the
other hand, places them side by side, one concerned with class and the
other with ideology. Her critics argue that ideology, as an integral part
of any mode of production, can only be understood through an analysis
of the mode of production as a totality.

It is in relation to her use of Lacan that critics of Mitchell acknowl-
edge the debt they owe her as well as take issue with her, by pointing to
the intrusion of patriarchal assumptions in Lacan's theory.

Freud, Lacan and feminist theory

It is appropriate, then, to move to Lacan's shifting of the Freudian paradigm from a neurophysiological or biological model, to the extent that it
was for Freud, to the level of social construction; this he does through
indicating the importance of language for society and for social subjecthood. He shifts the focus to the realm of the symbolic and redefines the
two significant moments at the pre-Oedipal and Oedipal stages referred
to earlier. These are now conceptualised as the entry into the Imaginary
order and the Symbolic order.[4]

For Lacan the human animal is turned into a subject by submission to
language, to the world of difference and especially sexual difference. The

pre-Oedipal phase is the realm of the Imaginary and the Oedipal the realm of the Symbolic, with the introduction of the use of language.

This first stage is what is referred to as the mirror-stage. For Lacan, the mirror-stage indicates that the ego develops, essentially, in alienation. That is, the child mis-recognises itself in the image—whether this be the mother's face or someone else's or every face it comes across. This stage takes in the period, approximately, from six months to 21 months. It is called the mirror-stage because, whereas an animal when placed in front of a mirror will look behind it and pat it and so on, but will eventually become bored and stop playing with it, the human child has an endless fascination for it, and will play appearing and disappearing games. The child recognises (mis-recognises) itself in it. At this stage the ego and the world are one; and at the same time absence of the mother—or the disappearance of the image—has to be managed. This is where Lacan introduces the concept of desire, which is intimately bound up with lack. He replaces Freud's instincts, or drives, with this concept of desire—whether for the mother's breast or for her presence or for the general wishing to be total, complete. This is the first stage when desire (and lack) have to be managed.

So at the mirror-stage, the first recognition is mis-recognition: hence 'man's ego is for ever irreducible to his lived identity' (Lacan, cited in Roussel, 1968:74). This is clearly a critical point in the integration of psychoanalytic theory and theories of ideology which rely on this idea of living-in-ideology, of mis-recognition. It should be stressed at this point that Lacan is more interested than many of his critics in the insights from other fields and it is fundamental to his theory that we are born 'prematurely' (Lacan, 1968b:74)—and that it is this helplessness of the human infant which in large part explains the period during which the unformed individual seeks to know her/himself through the image of another, or the Other. Lacan is criticised here, for a certain biologism, as he is for phallocentrism at a later stage. I can only say that I would like to reserve judgment in relation to the former. (See Timpanaro, 1974, 1975).

This dyadic, or unbroken tie—identification with the Other as one-self—can only be broken by the intervention of a third element, and this is the Symbolic order. Here Lacan relies on Lévi-Strauss's conception of the rule, as the inauguration of culture. The Symbolic order is the order of language. The connection between language and the unconscious is an essential part of Lacan's theory. Lacan indicates that the primary processes operating in the unconscious are themselves indistinguishable from fundamental linguistic mechanisms: condensation is the field of metaphor, and displacement is that 'veering off of meaning that we see in metonymy' (Lacan, 1972:305). This fact, that the unconscious is structured like a language, is not, in this account, related to inherent structures of the mind. It arises through the relation between the unconscious and language at the point of entry into the Symbolic order. The essential part of Lacan's account here is the central role that the phallus plays—as key signifier of lack, and as the universal signifier of human desire. The castration complex is not analysed in terms of the loss or feared loss of the penis, but in terms of the phallus. When he insists that the phallus is the universal signifier of lack, he is also shifting the emphasis from the empirical knowledge which the child gains that the mother lacks a penis and that the father has one, and the different ways in which girls and boys manage this and the resulting Oedipal drama and its resolution. He transfers the problem to the level of the Symbolic order—the level of language. Using the insights developed in structural linguistics, particularly those of de Saussure (1960), who established that language was only made up of differences, and that meaning only existed according to the relations of differences contracted in a chain of signifiers, the phallus assumes importance in this respect—as the signifier of all signifiers in fact; the key signifier of lack, of difference, of desire. Now Lacan insists that in his theory the phallus is not equated with the penis, and indeed, strictly it cannot be, since a signifier is marked by its lack. But in his account, in the playing out of the Oedipal drama, this lack is experienced by both girls and boys in their different ways, through the castration complex. This is the significant moment of breaking the closed relationship with the mother and of taking on a feminine or masculine identity in relation to both mother and father. The phallus appears to symbolise the penis in his account: it is identified with it to the important extent that the entry into the Symbolic order is overlaid by the Oedipal phase and its resolution through the castration complex.

Following Freud, Lacan does not differentiate according to gender in the first phase, but by accepting the necessity of the castration complex, he too, universalises the law of the father. Althusser puts Lacan's position more clearly than Lacan in this respect, when he says of the central role that the phallus plays: 'this may seem astonishing or arbitrary, but all psycho-analysts attest to it as a fact of experience' (Althusser, 1978c:213).

There are various criticisms that can be made of Lacan. The first and most obvious is this: to attribute to the phallus such a central role only makes sense in a system within which it is valorised. To assume it is universally valorised is to assume from the outset patriarchy, rather than establishing whether or not the processes by which an individual enters the social order can occur through neutral signifiers. That is, it excludes from discussion whether or not an individual can become part of a symbolic order within which the coding structure is not pointing to, or making central, signifiers that are already expressions of power, of domination and subordination. The question is, is this necessarily—'eternally'—a prerequisite for social subjecthood.

Jacka (1977) has argued that Lacan does not take into account the pre-language mechanisms for social identity, and in particular, those of gender allocation. By conflating language with the symbolic order he cannot distinguish gender at the pre-Oedipal phase. Language can, retrospectively, order prelinguistic experiences, and these experiences, from the moment of birth and even preceding it, are important considerations for a complete understanding of gender allocation, and the differences that emerge between the sexes (Jacka, 1977:310).

To summarise briefly the last few points: critics of Mitchell, Freud and Lacan are concerned to point out that there is a symbolic order already serving to form the infant before language is acquired. The process of gender identity is part of the moment of primary repression which precedes the Oedipal phase and is only retrospectively given social meaning through language. Lacan, then, is criticised for his phallocentrism, which rests on the presumed universality of the Oedipus (castration) complex; and this is related to his other problem, his conflation of the symbolic order with the acquisition of language, which leads him to neglect the importance of pre-linguistic symbolic interaction. It should be pointed out, though, that Lacan speaks of the Oedipus complex *or its equivalent*. He says:

> Obviously the Oedipus complex can only appear in a patri-archal form of the institution of the family—but it has no less contestable value as a threshold and I am convinced that in those cultures which exclude it, the function must have been fulfilled . . . by initiation experiences. (Wilden, citing Lacan, 1968a:126)

That is, since he insists the phallus is not the same as the penis, the phallus is the universal signifier of lack even where the Oedipus complex does not occur. Following Freud, he equates initiation (meaning circumcision) with castration, with subjection to the law of the father (Freud, 1940 (1959):58). It is precisely the variability between cultures that seems important here, and particularly for feminist analyses.

It could be argued that it is only in social formations where structural relations of domination and subordination are required that such a process exists. It may not be social subjecthood that requires the Oedipal drama or the castration complex, but a particular form of social subjecthood. Campioni, for example, though holding that '*primal repression* and the *castration complex*' are 'the points of contact between the Marxist theory of ideology and psychoanalysis' (Campioni, 1976b:36), maintains that only the first of these can be accepted as a universal feature of society. The castration complex involves a certain specific content in the unconscious for which, in her view, no such general claim can be made. Campioni sees a fundamental connection between the inferior status of women and class relations of domination and subordination (1976b:54). She argues that the very acceptance of relations of domination/subordination rests on the 'inferiorising' of women, the castration complex being a precondition. The aptness of her analysis, as she says, is 'best demonstrated in the capitalist mode of production'. This is no doubt a reflection, in part, of the fact that both class analysis and psychoanalysis have developed under capitalism. But it is clear that we need to know more of social formations other than our own, as well as knowing more about the variability within our own, both in the present and over time. Though Campioni's formulation is not sufficiently elastic, as it stands, to encompass the variously manifested forms of female subordination in social formations not constituted by classes, it does offer the means of 'explaining' patriarchy in materialist terms. To assert that it is *eternal*, would be, in this view, to assert that all social formations, in order to exist, require relations of domination/subordination. If one believes, with Campioni, that this is not the case, one could, if need be, accept evidence of universal patriarchy through human history without implicitly accepting the need for resignation to its unending future perpetuation. One could also argue from this perspective, that in social formations where relations of domination/subordination are not based on gender, the Oedipus complex may not, necessarily, exist. Domination–subordination relations cannot be equated with male–female relations, as is frequently the case (cf. Campioni, 1976b).

Fanon (1970), for instance, argues that it is not the father but the colonial power which is the source of repression and anxiety and that the Oedipus complex does not exist in his patients. (Fanon is referring here to the clinical situation). He also argues that the black man is the source of fear as well: in dream analysis, for instance, the castration threat seems to come from the imposition of the white interpretation of the world to which all colonised peoples are subjected, and the black man is the source of fear to white people. This locates the process very much into a specific social and political milieu: the father = political and economic and psychological power. The plausibility of his schema is perhaps indicative of the problem associated with psychoanalytic approaches to issues of domination and subordination: strict and logical methods combined with what appears as rigorous theorising are employed to construct variant theses which are in fact based on speculations about the 'scientific', valid, or generally applicable nature of Freud's theories. Moreover, the arguments frequently imply that the unconscious in the Freudian sense has a more profound effect on individuals than the 'living-in-ideology' of everyday life.

Conclusions

As I have said earlier, it seems necessary to me to make a clear distinction between the unconscious of Freud's theory, or reconstructions of this, and the 'mis-recognition' or 'living-in-ideology' which is a permanent feature of the social world and is not 'unconsciously' lived in the same way. Apart from the different meanings of the word 'unconscious' in these two contexts, the use of the word in the latter context has involved a form of structuralism which has become quite popular among some Marxists.[5] The structures underlying social reality are not of the same order as the 'invisible' content of Freud's unconscious. Although it is true that one can get at this content through analysis of its distorted representations, the implication of the analogy is that the same process applies at the social level. This type of approach neglects the transparency of the underlying structures of the social world and the extent of recognition of mis-recognition that occurs at different levels. This is what class struggle and feminist political intervention are all about. People's responses to the world are more complex, contradictory and perceptive of underlying processes than many of these theories would lead us to believe.

In this context, I believe that Althusser's notion of relative autonomy is useful when stripped of its functionalist overtones, but has been abused by many people who have applied it. It is integrally bound up with the concept of over-determination and cannot be understood apart from it. Althusser was more aware than many of his followers of the dangers of transposing some of these concepts; however, he found Freud's concept of over-determination useful for understanding the relationship between different levels of a social formation. The term 'over-determination' is an appropriate one to understand the very complex ways in which the ideological, political and economic levels of a social formation are linked up with each other. Mitchell incorrectly simplifies this to a 'complex notion of "multiple causation" in which the

Subordination

numerous factors can reinforce, overlap, cancel each other out, or contra-
dict one another—a very different proposition from that suggested by
simple determinism' (1975:309).

As with Freud's interminable analysis, it is again in the last instance
that a particular complex of practices or events determines the total
outcome:

> Not only are the elements of a dream determined by the
> dream-thoughts many times over, but the individual dream-
> thoughts are represented in the dream by several elements.
> Associative paths lead from one element of the dream to
> several dream-thoughts, and from one dream-thought to
> several elements of the dream. Thus a dream is not con-
> structed by each individual dream-thought, or group of
> dream-thoughts, finding (in abbreviated form) separate rep-
> resentation in the content of the dream ... a dream is
> constructed, rather, by the whole mass of dream-thoughts
> being submitted to a sort of manipulative process in which
> those elements which have the most numerous and strongest
> supports acquire the right of entry into the dream-content
> ... the elements of the dream are constructed out of the
> whole mass of dream-thoughts and each one of those
> elements is shown to have been determined many times over
> in relation to the dream-thoughts. (Freud, 1976:389)

Althusser's notion of relative autonomy has given a licence to people
who want to develop 'regional' theories and in fact to treat levels as
completely autonomous. This is quite reasonable if these theorists believe
that they *are* completely autonomous; but what has occurred is the
development of fields, or work within fields such as semiotics and
psychoanalysis, which are described as regional theories within that of
historical materialism, although the connection with the latter is for
some only nominal. For instance, the connection with class, class
structure and class struggle is frequently omitted. The importance of the
early criticisms of Mitchell's work lies there: while she disconnected
patriarchal ideology from class, there was an insistence that both were
historically specific and are only understood together. Hence the need to
be more specific about what patriarchy meant, and what forms women's
subordination took, and whether it was always an appropriate
description of the ideology of the social formation in question.

The insistence on eliminating biologism, phallocentrism, essentialism,
idealism, and so on, has been one which frequently calls for their permanent elimination.[6] The anti-reductionist stance associated with an

historical materialist approach has involved a ruthless examination of ideological or taken-for-granted assumptions. Freud's and Lacan's decentring of the subject so the focus is less on the ego, the conscious individual, and more on processes of which the individual is unaware, is important. But to take away the fact that she/he is biologically constructed as well runs the risk of yet another form of idealism (see Timpanaro, 1974, 1975; Cockburn, 1981). This, coupled with the centrality placed on language, on modes of discourse, also runs the risk of forgetting the extent to which these are situated in particular sociohistorical contexts, the importance of which initiated this sort of program in the first place.

Psychoanalysis is an important area for understanding the taking on of gender identity and is therefore important to feminist theory. But while the process of subjecthood is understood to be historically and socially specific, we have indeed a chicken-and-egg situation. An appeal to change attitudes is to assume a consciousness-centred individual, but an appeal to change the content of the unconscious is equally untenable. We are left again to change practices, which determine to such a large extent the attitudes we hold. Social arrangements in need of reorganisation were highlighted by the feminist analyses of Freudian theory and the practice of psychoanalysis. It is to these social arrangements—for example, the separation of men from childcare, the division of labour within the family, the patterns of occupational segregation within the labour market—that further work needs to be directed.

The family as a site for the reproduction of male–female relationships derives its importance from its connection with these other social and economic arrangements. Feminist theorists, previously intensely interested in the family at the expense of its connections with other social institutions, are proceeding with an examination of the dynamics of the relationships which exist between it and the school as well as the workplace. What goes on within the family can be better understood when located in this wider setting.

6

An extended theory of social reproduction

This chapter broadens the scope of inquiry into 'the tenacity of sexual assymetry and inequality' (Chodorow, 1978:6). The preceding chapters have developed the theme that the situation of women is not to be accounted for simply in terms of the immediate economic requirements of a particular system. Shifting attention from modes of production to processes of social reproduction makes possible a more comprehensive study of the processes of gender construction and reconstruction.

Previous chapters have documented the accompanying shifts of focus from the family to a range of other social institutions as primary sites for women's subordinate status. We need now to develop an understanding of processes of gender construction as they are sustained by the institutions of the state, the education system and the family.

It is important to emphasise that an examination of these processes cannot proceed without also accounting for the class structure. Gender and class are so inextricably linked that neither assumes a primary or determining place.

Feminist theory and the state

It would be tempting to discuss contemporary forms of the state solely in relation to women and then, more particularly, to focus on social policies which affect women and families. These do seem the clearest expressions of the ways in which women's lives are affected by state activity. But this would be a limited analysis. We have also to take account of a range of activities which do not appear, on the surface of things, to be policies affecting women and the work they perform within the family.

The state is not a thing; it does not exist as a single, monolithic entity. It is a complex of relationships, embodying a certain form of power operating through various institutional arrangements. The state has been a concern of the feminist movement since its beginning; theories of the state are implicit in the strategies of the feminist movement. The original demands of Women's Liberation groups in Britain, Australia and North America centred around state provision of childcare, equal pay, availability of contraception and abortion and equality of opportunity in employment and education.

The state is a social-political process, the result at any given moment of struggles and demands such as these feminist demands. Feminist political activity, though, does not necessarily represent the interests of working-class women. Success within the institutions of the state implies a certain degree of power, so that 'middle-class' women's demands are more readily formulated, put forward and negotiated. But it is certain that feminist activity has had an impact on state policy. The original demands of the feminist movement have to some extent been met by the provision of childcare centres, women's health centres, women's refuges, rape crisis centres, repeal of anti-abortion laws, the development of equal employment programs. Attempts to cut back on these services are sharply resisted.

Some writings argue that the state determines family life as the instrument of a patriarchal, class order, but such accounts of the state often neglect the extent to which feminist activity has had an effective influence:

> [P]ower and legal authority are never, even in their most alienated forms, a one-directional force. Any under-class, no matter how oppressed, is capable of having its needs and interests recognized and given formal legal expression to some degree. (Fraser, 1976:155)

Within feminist theory, there was an early concentration on the welfare aspects of the state at the expense of understanding, in historical terms, how the state, through juridical and other arrangements, continued to define women, and contributed to the definitions of masculinity and femininity in ways not immediately obvious.

Elizabeth Wilson's *Women and the Welfare State* (1977) is an example of a concentration on the welfare face of the state in relation to women. In this and in an earlier article, 'Women and the Welfare State' (1974) Wilson makes her concern with state activity in relation to the regulation of sexuality clear. In her terms, the very definition of femininity is a concern of the state: 'the Welfare State is not just a set of services, it is also a set of ideas about society, about the family, and—not least important—about women' (Wilson, 1977:9).

Wilson distinguishes two aspects of the state's functioning: those to do with the law and those to do with welfare policy. Referring to Britain, she indicates that certain pieces of legislation such as the *Equal Pay Act* 1970 and the *Sex Discrimination Act* 1975 are dealing with the more obvious ways in which the pay structure and the law have discriminated against women. On the other hand, welfare provisions and social policies operate 'in a more subtle and in some ways a more coercive fashion' to continue to define women's primary adult task, that of reproducing the workforce.

Wilson attempts a textual analysis of the reports relating to the development of the welfare state in Britain, in particular, the Beveridge Report (1942) and the Newson Report on education, published as *Half Our Future* (1963).[1] She analyses the reports in terms of the vision of a 'just' society towards which they were directing policy. These documents give us many clues to the assumptions about women which were made in a period of active postwar reconstruction and Wilson ably demonstrates many of these. But, of course, they do not tell us how women responded, neither as young students at school, nor as wives, mothers and workers. There are many histories involved here which have yet to be documented. For example, little is known and understood of women's response to a changing definition of femininity after their active participation in the workforce during the war. After World War II, women were encouraged back into the home, having 'vital work to do in the adequate continuance of the British race' (Beveridge, 1942:43). Wilson provides a hint of how people might have responded. She refers to a study carried out by Slater and Woodside (1951) which found that the form of services and the amount of money by which parents were expected to carry out this task (and which involved, for many, the loss of the wife's income), were too meagre to constitute real incentives. They found 'that on the question of government propaganda to persuade couples to have more babies both the men and their wives showed "the strongest resentment"' (Wilson, 1977:141). Moreover, a study conducted for the Ministry of Reconstruction in 1943 by the Wartime Social Survey pointed out that

> half the married women aged over thirty-five years and almost one-third of those under thirty years of age said when interviewed that they wanted to stay in employment even after the war was over. Altogether 60 per cent of occupied women in 1943 wanted to work after the war. (Land, 1976:116)

The emphasis on analysing the welfare face of the state has led to conclusions about its increased 'intervention' in a previously 'private' sphere, that is, that of relationships within the family. Any suggestion that the state is interfering with the family more than it once did ignores the fact that, directly and indirectly, the intervention of the law in family life has been going on since before industrialisation. The definition of women in law, the consequences for ownership of property and children, legislation on female labour—in all these respects the state has moved back and allowed greater freedom. It is when placed in this wider context that we can begin to explore the implications of particular welfare interventions.

The intervention of the state by way of social welfare measures is highly selective. What it omits to do is as significant as the positive support it provides. The state 'defines a space, the family, in which its agents will not interfere but in which control is left to the man' (McIntosh, 1978:257), either formally, as in law, or implicitly, as a result of women's financial dependence. Although the situation is beginning to change in these respects, women are still denied adequate legal protection in cases of rape and domestic violence. Here the public/private ideology emerges again—'the assumption that women's contexts are too private and personal to be subject to criminal sanction leaves women exposed to violence and abuse' (McIntosh, 1978:258). This distinction has been closely examined within feminist theory in acknowledgement of the fact that ' "[p]rivate" needs are the individually mediated expression of determinate forms of social and historical experience and, as such, they possess an undeniably "public" character' (Fraser, 1976:155).

Most important, state welfare policies do nothing to alter the dependent status of married women. Wilson says that 'social welfare policies amount to no less than the *State organization of domestic life*' (1977:9). This is not to deny the importance of policies which are not welfare policies (but which bear immediately on family life), such as those concerned with the labour market. Many of these other policies assume a particular form of family household, predicated on a male wage and upon female domestic service (McIntosh, 1978:255). Such policies tend in fact to perpetuate the 'normal' household, since they impose economic penalties on households which depart from the pattern on which incomes policy, taxation policy and social security benefits are based.

Wilson's analysis of the relationship between welfare policies and the family, and her stress on the way in which welfare policies perpetuate women's dependent status, is carried on by McIntosh:

> [T]he social security system has worked in a curious way, on

the one hand to establish married women as dependent
upon their husbands (and therefore as not entirely reliant
upon wage labour) but on the other hand by restricting their
direct eligibility for social security benefits, to make them
more vulnerable to use as cheap labour power when they do
have to engage in wage labour. (McIntosh, 1978:264)

Welfare policies prescribe certain activities and outcomes. It is in analysing these that Wilson, and McIntosh after her, begin a fruitful analysis
of 'patriarchal' ideology as it is expressed through state activities. However, the concept of 'femininity' which the state promotes (Wilson,
1977:41) needs to be broken down and described and understood in its
different manifestations. In other words, state activity and its relation
to women cannot be analysed as if all women are affected in the same
way. A class analysis of the differential effects of state activity on
women needs to be made. Similarly, the influence of feminist activity
and class conflict on state policies must be accounted for in an adequate
historical account of the state.

The relation of women of different classes to state activities is better
understood by examining state regulation of the labour market than by
the analysis of social policy. Social policy is, in the main, simply dealing
with the effects of the labour market. The history of family allowances
in Britain and Australia illustrates the point admirably. The significance of these allowances clearly lies in their reinforcement of the
importance of male wage labour, rather than their ostensible purpose of
providing support for children (Land, 1976; McIntosh, 1978). The
family allowance is a social security benefit which is integrally tied up
with taxation and wages policy. The links between these have varied
over time, depending on trade union pressure (for increases in and different versions of a family wage, for instance), feminist pressure (for
family allowances to be paid directly to the mother) or government pressure to change all these relationships both by pegging the payment at a
level which does not undermine the (male) incentive to work, while
serving also as a justification for wage restraint.[2]

The preceding analysis draws our attention to the need to be clear
about the direction in which policies should be reformed or developed.
Existing taxation, wages and social security policies in Britain, Australia
and the United States reinforce the connections between the segregated
occupational structure and the sexual division of labour within the
family. They *all* combine to perpetuate women's dependence on the
state or on their husbands and their susceptibility to poverty.

A leverage point for feminist political intervention lies in putting pressure on governments to reform these policies to reflect the shifts in practices signalled by anti-discrimination legislation. Many writers have shown how taxation, wages and social security policies, historically, have served different interests, sought different ends. They have also shown how, although broadly intended to promote economic growth and stability, such policies have revealed contradictory attitudes to men and women, to workers and the unemployed, and to the family. The net effects have been the persistence of the dependent status of women and the lowering of the value of the wage.

The point in examining these policies is to clarify how they should be reformed and to what ends. Feminist analysis leads to the conclusion that the principle underlying reform is that through all these policies, women should be treated as separate and independent persons, regardless of marital or employment status. Further, no policy which affects women's financial status should disadvantage lower income groups generally.

At present, many social policies are ambiguously formulated. Those which are explicitly directed towards the protection of mothers and children at the same time penalise them, particularly when these people are not in nuclear family settings. Policies may accept the realities of women's paid employment and of changing household patterns and thereby compensate households within which there are juvenile, invalid or retired dependants—that is, gear benefits to individuals in need; or, on the other hand, policies may penalise people outside traditional modes and provide advantages to the nuclear family type with one (male) breadwinner. At the moment in Australia, the latter is the case, although the advantages go only to those whose sole income is relatively high.

State activity maintains a particular type of household—male breadwinner, dependent spouse and children. But it does not do this in any mechanistic way, nor solely for the purpose of oppressing women. It certainly does it in accord with prevailing assumptions about women which many would prefer to leave unquestioned. But these assumptions are perpetuated by the ways in which women are constrained to organise their lives, given the limited choices possible within the framework imposed by state policies. As McIntosh observes, '[w]omen living with husbands or male sexual partners are assumed by the state to be dependent upon them (and so either *are* dependent on them or are forced to work at, possibly, very disadvantageous rates of pay)' (1978:281).

But state encouragement of traditional household patterns has not been altogether successful. In fact, despite the way in which social security systems tend to define women as dependent, in recent years there has been an enormous increase in the number of households headed by females. In a search for independence, some women are prepared to risk the poverty into which single parenthood may throw them.

These changes in women's reliance for themselves and their dependants on earned income have implications for tax structures. The main issues, as Edwards presents them (1980a:7) are first, the relevance of marriage to taxation; second, the effect dependent children have on the ability of their parent(s) to pay tax; third, the difference in tax paid by one-income and two-income households; and fourth, the tax treatment of the unemployed.[3]

The relevance of marriage to personal taxation policy in Australia is expressed in the tax rebate given for a dependent spouse. An examination conducted by Edwards (1980a) of this rebate together with other aspects of taxation policy directed to the family, revealed some absurd assumptions about marriage as against, for instance, parenthood.

The question which Edwards poses is whether (and if so, to what extent), our tax structure should provide a subsidy on marriage to a couple, one of whom chooses to stay at home. The rebate presupposes that marriage affects people's ability to pay tax and/or to earn income. It also presupposes a just distribution of income within the family, or between husband and wife (for preliminary findings which dispute this assumption, see Edwards, 1980b).

The rebate helps neither single parents nor parents with childcare expenses. The benefit is confined to the traditional family; it is a policy which discriminates in favour of this family type and it neglects to take into account the existing diversity of household arrangements. In this respect it is coercive legislation, eliminating or reducing options, in particular, the work incentive for women.

The assumptions underlying the policy are summarised by Edwards:

> the size of the rebate compared to the value of family allowances implies that there is more economic significance in marriage than there is in parenthood; in addition, our tax structure assumes that child-care expenses do not exist, and that a sole parent's ability to pay tax is greater than that of a married taxpayer (1980a:20).

A mother in paid employment not only derives no benefit from the dependent spouse rebate, but is not even entitled to claim childcare costs as an expense in earning income. Taxation policy recognises marriage when there is usually no change in a couple's earning capacity on marriage. But children are not only a significant financial cost in themselves, they affect the earning capacity of one parent—either through the loss of one income or through payment for childcare. Parenthood is massively more expensive than marriage unless, of course, marriage is only regarded as a state in which women are totally dependent on men.

While parenthood has a marked effect on the ability to pay tax, the tax system does not distinguish tax-paying parents from other types of taxpayer except in the provision of a tax rebate for sole parents, introduced in Australia in 1975. The change from a tax rebate for dependent children to the provision of family allowances takes this payment, strictly speaking, outside the taxation system. This point merely reinforces the argument that wages, taxation and social security policies are interconnected in ways not necessarily acknowledged by those who implement them.

The dependent spouse rebate increases women's dependence on their husbands. The unemployed spouse is not entitled to unemployment benefits. Taxation policy needs to treat an unemployed married person as an individual entitled to unemployment benefits in the same way as every other unemployed individual.

Such policy reforms are not merely issues of social justice, but are bound up with the circularity within which women's subordination is so apparently intractable. These policy initiatives are crucial leverage points in breaking the cycle of women's dependence and exploitation.

The state and biological reproduction

It is necessary to distinguish conceptually the different processes of reproduction with which the state is involved. But it is equally important to put them together again in the variable ways in which they happen to be connected in social practice at any given historical time. The state's involvement in processes of biological reproduction is not separate, in practice, from other processes of more general social reproduction. But we need to distinguish them and sort out their relationships in different economic and political circumstances.

Family size and population levels are influenced by state activity in different ways. The purpose of my comments is not to criticise policies of population control but rather to point to the necessity of discovering the ways in which women are differently affected by them. Family allowances, ideas about 'motherhood', industrial legislation affecting wage rates and women's employment, the provision or lack of provision of childcare facilities, ideas about acceptable standards of living, all affect birthrates and affect them differently at different points of the class structure. An interesting area for investigation would be to observe the unfolding of an apparent contradiction: in times of high unemployment such as now, the importance of 'mother at home' is revived while the idea of the male as breadwinner, coupled with the belief that women are taking men's jobs, takes increasing hold. The unemployment of married women is to a great extent hidden or partial. The movement back into the home in the past has been accompanied by a rise in the birthrate. The situation in Britain and Australia after World War II is not a good analogy here, as in the prevailing social and economic climate motherhood was encouraged in order to achieve a rise in the birthrate, and the particular contradiction then was that women were also needed to expand the labour force. The present contradiction, however, is to encourage women to be at home without necessarily being involved over a long period of time caring for young children. When women are relieved of childcare there is pressure on the market for paid employment. Australian governments have responded to the requirements of the labour market, and women's movement into the paid labour force, partly by manipulating immigration policy; this is an area within which there is still flexibility. But the extent to which women determine for themselves their reproductive and productive lives, and the constraints they experience, are matters which it would be particularly instructive to pursue during a time of economic crisis.

From the standpoint of the individual middle-class woman, it might appear that women have increased control over biological reproduction through the contraceptive means now available and the encouragement of family planning generally. Women are freer to choose if and when they will have children, and how many. Yet this perception ignores an historical process which in many important ways has taken away from women the freedom to make these decisions for themselves. This area used to be 'women's business', one within which women looked after other women, passed information on to each other and could, without interference from the law, restrict their family size through such techniques as they knew, including abortion and infanticide.

Oakley (1976) elaborates this point. She traces the process whereby 'professionalization has been accompanied by a transfer of control from women to men':

> The main change in the social and medical management of
> childbirth and reproductive care in industrialized cultures
> over the last century has been the transition from a struc-

ture of control located in a community of untrained women,
to one based on a profession of formally trained men.
(1976:18)

This is not to say that the professionalisation of childbirth and infant
care has been only a regressive step. It clearly has not, given lowered
mortality rates and the improved health of mothers and infants. Nevertheless, the fact remains that what appears to be an area of free choice
has increasingly been appropriated from women at a social and political
level (see Macintyre, 1976).

The outcome of this is that the involvement of women in childbirth
has been diminished to the irreducible biological act of producing babies.
All other aspects of the total situation have been increasingly profes-
sionalised and determined by law and by the medical profession. Innova-
tions relating to contraception, childbirth, pre- and postnatal care have
been elevated to the status of scientific and technological discourse, and
defined separately from women's experiences. Nevertheless, as Macintyre (1976) points out, 'normal' circumstances under which women
choose to have babies (i.e., within marriage) are redefined—and negotiated in relation to representatives of the medical profession—by the
women themselves.

The effects of exclusion processes on women in different classes can
be found here. Bertrand Russell 1929 (1961) discussed the ways in
which birth control literature has been distributed in the past, and the
different ways in which it was permissible to speak about it:

many subjects can be discussed in long technical words
known only to highly educated people, which cannot be
mentioned in any language understanded of the people . . .
[sic] Sometimes this prohibition of simple language has
grave consequences; for example, Mrs. Sanger's pamphlet on
birth control, which is addressed to working women, was
declared obscene on the grounds that working women could
understand it. Dr. Marie Stopes's books, on the other hand,
are not illegal, because their language can only be understood by persons with a certain amount of education. The
consequence is that, while it is permissible to teach birth
control to the well-to-do, it is criminal to teach it to wage-
earners and their wives. (Russell, 1961: 58-9).

Wilson (1977) points out the ways in which the contraceptive pill,
so far from being a 'liberating' innovation for all women, is actually
used as a form of social control of some. In Britain under the NHS
Family Planning Act (1967) 'contraceptives were to be widely distrib-

uted and were to be free for the poorest families ... This was an
attempt at a population policy and coincided with a renewed attack on
large "problem" families' (1977:69). That the Pill was a method of *controlling* women's sexuality can be seen in the Finer Report, to which
Wilson also refers. This report pointed out that there are three groups
of women with special needs in the matter of contraceptive advice: unmarried women, women who conceive before marriage, and those
married to unskilled workers (Wilson, 1977:70). Though Wilson's
assessment of the report may be too harsh, she rightly asks by whom
the pregnancies to be prevented are 'unwanted'. It is not at all clear that
the wishes of the women concerned are seen as paramount. Some of
these women may want to have children, but as a result of social attitudes and/or living conditions their children can readily be labelled
'unwanted'.

Biological reproduction and state intervention in its patterning must,
then, be distinguished from other aspects of social reproduction because
of its historical and social variability. However, as a social process it is
not separate from the processes by which the social relations of a particular social formation are reproduced. Again, state activity plays
a crucial role. Family law, industrial legislation, social policy relating to
good and bad parenthood, education policy, taxation policy and so on all
help to define the ways in which relationships between males and
females, adults and children are constructed. They all contribute to the
formation of particular types of 'masculinity' and 'femininity'.

Education and social reproduction

The education system is one of the most powerful ways in which the
state intervenes in the process of reproducing the social relations of production. The combined influence of gender and class at schools is a
central concern of feminist theory. It is in educational policy and practice and in responses to them that the perpetuation of women's familial
role may be more evident than in social policies directly relating to the
family.

School experience is a significant factor in the allocation of women to
particular kinds of work. The education system needs examination not
only on its own, but also in relation to the family, which precedes and co-
exists with it. We need to consider also the education system's response
to changes in the demands of the market for female labour as well as
demands from the feminist movement. Both sets of pressures have led
to a great deal of public discussion as well as government enquiries and

reports. These documents reflect the conflicting pressures on the education system and call for both the elimination of discriminatory practices within the schools and the training of females 'realistically' to fit into their adult roles.

Feminist theory and practice have acknowledged that the school plays some part in the reproduction of female subordination. The education system has been attacked for its explicitly sexist content as well as the 'hidden curriculum' of the schools. But this criticism has remained largely separate from theorising about the family.[4] Similarly, the 'new' sociology of education is increasingly concentrating on the distribution and organisation of knowledge, culture and ideology, with respect to the reproduction of the class structure (and of the working class in particular), at the expense of male–female relations.[5] These perspectives need to be drawn together. An adequate theory of the connections between the several reproduction processes requires empirical investigation.

Social reproduction entails a legitimising process. The 'equality of opportunity' ideology has been undermined through a recognition that 'even among the population at large . . . social force is exercised in the form of economic exchange, [and that] the market has lost its credibility as a fair . . . mechanism for the distribution of life opportunities' (Habermas, 1976:81). Many writers have argued that an ideology of 'merit' has taken its place as a legitimising theme.[6] It refers to a standard of achievement, to an individual's efforts, determination and willingness combined with a notion of ability defined in relation to the needs of a technologically advanced society.

There has been another shift by which 'merit' comes increasingly to mean not just the achievement of formal credentials but the possession of a wider range of personal attributes—'non-cognitive personality traits'. The narrower meaning of the term appears less and less adequate a justification for the actual processes of selection for, and allocation of, social rewards:

> [F]ar wider ranges of the child's attributes become legitimate objects of evaluative scrutiny and explanatory variables in the construction of success and failure. Not merely intellectual but social, emotional, aesthetic and even physical criteria are often employed in the processing of pupils in educational institutions, the social control possibilities thus being enhanced. (Sharp and Green, 1975:225)

This allows for a great deal of flexibility in relation to the occupational system. The connection between formal academic credentials suitable to particular jobs and the individuals holding these credentials is loosened by bringing personality characteristics into the assessment. It is here that 'femininity' may have a somewhat chequered, but never powerful, history.

Of course, this process has always existed, but it is now becoming institutionalised within the schools and the workplace.[7] In the work of Bowles, Gintis and Meyer (1974-75, 1975, 1975-76) this process is linked directly to the demands for appropriate personal skills in different segments of the labour market. As the content of ideology changes—the sets of ideas which are actively promoted to legitimise, or make sense of, the allocation of opportunities—there occur changes in social practices concerned with conveying knowledge of the social world.

Feminist theorising about these processes was, for a time, strongly influenced by Althusser's notes on ideology, 'Ideology and Ideological State Apparatuses' 1971 (1978b).[8] He argued that there are multiple ideological state apparatuses including the media, trade unions, political parties, schools, churches and the family. They are defined as part of the state because of their contribution to social cohesion on behalf of it (see also Poulantzas, 1972:251; 1975:51, 53-56). But it seems to me to make more sense to regard the family as a prime target for the state's activities, thus leaving room for an analysis of the contradictions, mediations and struggles which occur between them. This is not to deny that contradictory processes also occur among state institutions, as the discussion of the education system demonstrates. The characterisation of the family as an ideological state apparatus also obscures the relationship of the repressive, juridical aspect of the state in relation to familial relationships: through marriage and divorce laws, policies in relation to the welfare of children, and the provision and withdrawal of 'welfare' benefits, depending upon the circumstances involved. Of his list of 'ideological state apparatuses', the education system is the only one I am prepared to accept as belonging there, at least for those social formations, such as Britain and Australia, where education is, for most of the population, organised, developed and provided by governments.

Althusser was useful, too, in his insistence on the need to recognise that ideology has a material existence. Social relationships and activity are ideologically constructed and serve to conceal their own (ideological) nature. This is an important point in an analysis of social reproduction which focuses on ideology, as this cannot be regarded as a set of ideas separate from social practice.

There is a further criticism to be made of Althusser's scheme. In his account of the hierarchy of ideas, actions, practices, rituals, institutions and apparatuses, he says, '[a]n ideology always exists *in* an apparatus'

(1978b:166, my emphasis). Althusser does not account for the mediations and contradictions among apparatuses and institutions. He might be right in pointing to the family-school complex as the main site for reproducing the social relations of production. But from a feminist perspective it is more important to seek out the contradictions in the relationship between these, than it is to analyse the family-school as a single complex, in which each apparently reinforces the other in providing suitably disposed people for the labour market. I will be returning to this point.

The other main criticism of Althusser's notes has to do with his assertion that each ideological apparatus always performs a 'function' for capital 'in the way proper to it' (1978b:154). This empiricist statement confounds form and function. It takes for granted that the schools 'educate' and the family 'socialises' in particular ways which slot into each other in a manner suitable for the reproduction of the class structure. The empiricist method defines institutions by their apparent functions and it is presumed that distinct institutions are necessary to carry out distinct functions (Godelier, 1975:4). We *believe* that the schools 'educate' because that is their manifest function. Althusser divides the social world into its institutional manifestations and assumes correspondence as well as automatic reinforcement in relation to social reproduction. It is difficult, then, to see what else schools do, and, moreover, what other practices, outside the formal education system, 'educate' in the same way—in the broad sense of imparting knowledge about the social world.

The family-school complex is a vital arena for the social reproduction of 'masculinity' and 'femininity'. This is not so much because the family and the education system *are* the only pedagogical institutions but because it is *believed* that they are. It is not only the family, or the school, as particular institutions that continue the process of social reproduction, but also the powerful ideology of the family and of the educational system, as places for socialisation and learning. The power of the ideas of appropriate familial and educational processes inform parents' and teachers' practices.

The work of Bowles, Gintis and Meyer concentrates on the 'legitimation' function of the schools. The title of one of their articles makes clear where they are situating the education system: 'The long shadow of work . . .'—focusing on the sweeping effect of the requirements of capitalist production through the schools and the family.

They point to a complex relationship between work, the school and the family. On the one hand they recognise that a structural correspondence cannot be attributed to these institutions, for the family is seen as a refuge from precisely those impersonal and formally organised characteristics of the workplace and the school. On the other hand they argue that the experience of family members in the workforce is drawn into the values and modes of behaviour within the family, so that it becomes, despite itself, yet another prop for the class structure. But because of its difference in structure, the importance of the school is magnified: it is seen in their account as an important mediating structure, within which children from families are prepared for their future work experiences. In this respect the family is seen, on its own, as deficient or inadequate for performing this role: hence the importance of 'education' within the schools. The family is brought into the analysis in the first place because, despite the processes delineated within the schools, there remains a strong independent association between family background and economic success, although the children of more privileged parents tend also to receive more education (Bowles et al., 1974/5:17).

Bowles, Gintis and Meyer point to the distinction between paid and unpaid work within the family, its association with males and females respectively and the ways in which children in the family situation, by observation, identification and the internalisation of the 'appropriate' sex-role, perpetuate this pattern for themselves: 'the family's impact on the reproduction of the sexual division of labour is distinctly greater than that of the educational system' (1974–75:18). Second, this division of labour between males and females, which is a result of the capitalist process of production, involves the parents' self-concepts being formed in relation to this division, so that the mother, who defines herself as household worker, passes this differential sex-role typing on to her children in that additional way.

In their analysis, Bowles and his co-authors do not deal with the ambivalence people might consciously feel about their involvement in these institutions, and they deal inadequately with the unconscious aspects of the 'socialisation' process, not just within the family but also within the school. They ask the question, 'Under what conditions will individuals accept the pattern of social relations that frame their lives?' (1974–75:5) and they give the following alternatives: they may actively embrace such conditions; they may accept them with some resignation; they may passively submit with or without some vision of the possibilities of change of the system, and therefore seek individual solutions. Here people are depicted as responding in a fairly clear-cut way, and fairly passively—in the sense of not actively seeking out and creating new directions for themselves.

A further inadequacy of the work of Bowles and his associates is that they view the family as an institution which moulds individual consciousness before the school does. This leads them to emphasise the work-school and the family-work connections (particularly in relation to the wage-earner in the family—the father) at the expense of the family-school connection (which would draw the mother into the analysis in an important way). When they argue that 'the social relations of the educational encounter are predicted on prior experience in family life' (1974/5:4) they ignore the importance of the interaction between these two institutions.

Their concept of 'structural correspondence' between the workplace and the school, in terms of hierarchical arrangements and dominant-subordinate relationships also needs to be modified. It emphasises the structuring of the institution at the expense of the content of the social practices that are occurring within it. This is important, because some analyses of progressive educational techniques, or progressive schools, have shown that, despite the difference in structural organisation, especially to the extent that relations of domination and subordination have been consciously modified, the class structure nevertheless can be reinforced and supported in more subtle ways. (See, for instance, Sharp and Green, 1975). The consequences of such an assumption can be seen, for example, in attempts to change the *form* of the family from a nuclear one, or the form of the school, as efforts to avoid the pitfalls of the 'normal' arrangement, so that children will change in appropriate ways.

However, these innovative institutions are operating in a social milieu which places limits on their effectiveness. Further, the participants are carrying around with them the results of their own upbringing and their allocation in the social/sexual division of labour. Parents' and teachers' appreciation of boys and girls are undoubtedly coloured by the images of maleness and femaleness around them, through the ways in which production and work—paid and unpaid—are organised.

Parents and teachers are constantly adjusting to economic realities. In the 1950s and 1960s they could assume that their children and students would find employment should they choose to (if female) or because they had to (if male). Further education for its own sake was a workable option for those who could afford it. Education during the 1970s and 1980s is increasingly geared both to vocations and to the possibility of unemployment. There is pressure on schools to teach students how to comport themselves and how to dress when being interviewed for jobs. This competitive process potentially reinforces traditional notions of femininity (built into some jobs, such as that of receptionist) and facilitates a breaking away from it as women will increasingly, when seeking employment, broaden their options. All of this depends partly, of course, on the effectiveness of equal opportunity programs and anti-discrimination practices, to be discussed later. This is all part of the process of social reproduction. How children are brought up is not only part of the reproduction of the social relations of production (and in particular the social/sexual division of labour) but of the totality, which includes the structuring of masculinity and femininity as well as the structuring of classes, at one and the same time.

Feminist literature has begun to consider the impact on children of the contradictions so clearly pointed to in relation to women. What are the processes through which children consciously—as against unconsciously, or as against their implicit understandings of their social world—make decisions about the direction their lives will take? Children are observers, and make their own judgments about the viability or success of the options taken by people around them. How are the tensions between conformity (and acceptance) and non-conformity in relation to masculinity and femininity managed or dealt with by children? Children are required to negotiate, mediate and compromise in response to the constant pressures on them, and sometimes quite consciously separate their 'public' and 'private' selves. The literature concerned with the interior of the family—the work of Laing (1972), Laing and Esterson (1970) and Cooper (1971) in particular—and our knowledge of the dynamics operating in the relationships within which the small child is reared, are most informative here. The micro-processes occurring within the household are transferred to the macro-level of society, in the contradictory and ambiguous ways to which Mitchell (1971:146-47) draws attention.

Social processes which question traditional forms of masculinity and femininity bring shifts in character formation, and may validly lead to optimism. But their effects remain contestable. Besides, there are 'adjustment' processes carried out by parents and teachers designed to bring up children vaguely to 'fit', for *their* sake. We need to consider these 'accommodative strategies' on the part of children as well, and also the paradoxical outcomes of strategies designed to overcome apparent obstacles to taking up new opportunities. These strategies, to which I now turn, relate to gender and class at one and the same time. It is in an examination of people's efforts to change their life circumstances that we can demonstrate most clearly the class–gender relationship.

There are two works in particular with a focus on gender and class which attempt to come to grips with the activity of individuals and families aimed at changing or taking control over life opportunities. In both works, the education system is viewed as playing a central role in the development of these strategies. Paul Willis, in *Learning to Labour: how working class kids get working class jobs* (1977) and R.W. Connell and associates, in *Making the Difference: schools, families and social division* (1982) attempt to trace the relationships between school, family and the labour market, with particular reference to gender and class.

Willis focused on a segment of the male working class, and traced the development of particular manifestations of 'masculinity' on the part of these males. He chose a group of twelve 'non-academic working-class lads' typical of the working class in an industrial area in England and from a school exclusively working-class in intake. The group was compared with another group of boys from the same year at the same school, described as conformers, whose response to the contradictory demands on them is regarded by the lads as 'effeminate'. Both sets of responses can be described as strategies. Willis indicates that for the lads an exaggeration of masculinity was one element of their response to a class-structured situation within which they were excluded from the resources of others around them. The relationship between the masculinity of these boys and their perception of their life chances is a complex one and is more accurate than their teachers would admit (but one in which they played a significant part). Their masculinity is expressed as a reaction against the aims and expectations of the school. It emphasises manual work as against 'effeminate' mental labour and is combined with a celebratory opposition to authority, and an attitude towards females as both sexual objects and domestic comforters (Willis, 1977:43). These elements were expressed collectively, a collective assertion of masculinity, its legitimacy and power, constructed in the face of powerlessness in other aspects of their lives. Willis locates this particular manifestation of masculinity within the 'counter school' culture, rather than seeing it as part of the repertoire available within the dominant school-society cultural code. He is aware, though, of its 'usefulness' for the reproduction of the capitalist order:

> Far from patriarchy and its associated values being an unexplained relic of previous societies, it is one of the very pivots of capitalism in its complex, unintended preparation of labour power and reproduction of the social order. It helps to provide the real human and cultural conditions which in their continuously deconstructed, reconstructed, fragile, uncertain, unintended and contradictory ways

actually allow subordinate roles to be taken on 'freely'
within liberal democracy (1977:151).

The very masculinity the lads seek is part of the process of exclusion
from other forms of power. Similarly, the conformists, too, are acting
strategically. They have given up one form of power (provided in this
construction of masculinity) for another: the chance to rise in the class
structure *as they perceive it*. While mental labour is associated with
femininity, or at least is regarded as effeminate, it is also work that
'middle class' people perform. Here we observe the ambiguity in the
socially dominant construction of 'maleness'.

Willis's treatment of the problem is relevant to feminist theory in at
least two ways. It points to the *variable* construction of gender. His
analysis also makes clear that 'femininity' in a patriarchal order is a construction, in part, which is a *response* to the ways in which 'masculinity'
is constructed, and cannot be understood separately from it. Females
are remarkable in this book by their absence, but their brief appearances
make this point clear (Willis, 1977:43–47).

The problem left unresolved by Willis is why the particular manifestations of masculinity are produced as expressions of rebellion and conformity. Their suitability to capitalist production is described but not
explained. In fact, Willis is describing a process similar to that dealt
with by Sennett and Cobb (1973). Willis's lads, despite themselves,
end up locked into the prison of the shop floor (1977:107). Sennett's
and Cobb's men, too, attempted to change the lives of their children
through their belief in the education system, but were defeated by it
(1973:186–87).

Connell's idea of 'praxis traps' might usefully be brought in here,
'where people do things for good reason and skilfully, in situations that
turn out to make their original purpose impossible to achieve' (Connell,
1983:156). We are still left, though, with the task of explaining why
the result is one that tends to reproduce situations compatible with the
requirements for capital accumulation. As well, given our interest in
gender relations, we need adequate explanation of the 'enduring but
changing pattern of women's unequal access to economic security and
social autonomy' (Baldock and Class, 1983:xi).

The work of Connell and his associates is particularly appropriate to
discuss here, as this is one of the few books prepared to argue in a forth-
right fashion against the 'social reproduction' theorists—in which
category they place Willis—who, the authors believe, imply that 'most
people could not really understand what was happening to them. [Social
reproduction theory] suggested that they were blinded by ideology

(which was why they went on reproducing structures)' (Connell et al., 1982:28). This passage raises the crucial point: how does one explain the 'tenacity of sexual asymmetry' while at the same time according to individuals an active role in the construction of their own lives? Quite simply put, we are required to investigate not only women's active agency, but men's as well and the different capacities of different groups to effect fundamental social change. To argue that gender inequalities are reproduced is not to argue that there is a 'logic of reproduction'; Connell and associates are quite correct when they claim that '[i]f "reproduction" predominates in a given case, it is because that side of things has won out in a contest with other tendencies, not because it is guaranteed by some sociological law' (1982:190).

To claim that the reproduction of gender inequality is an outcome of strategies draws attention to the relevant arena—the structuring of power relationships in a capitalist society. *Making the Difference* is a report concerned with the 'interplay of school, family and workplace' (1982:9). The researchers investigated 100 14- and 15-year-olds, their parents, teachers and school principals. Half the families were of people doing manual or semi-manual work for wages, whose children attended government comprehensive schools in working-class suburbs. The other half were families of managers, business people and professionals, whose children attended independent, fee-charging schools. This book deserves close attention because it is, quite simply, one of the few that attends to class, gender and education. It is written by well-known researchers in the field in Australia and has had a considerable impact on educationists and scholars.

A major theme of the research emerged as the relations between the sexes: '[t]he evidence of the interviews is clear that this is quite a central issue for understanding the relations between families and schools in general; and for understanding the issue of class inequality in particular' (1982:33).

An important concept in the book is that of the 'hegemonic curriculum', its central feature being 'hierarchically-organised bodies of academic knowledge appropriated in individual competition', the effect of which is to marginalise other kinds of knowledge (1982:120).

Jules Henry (1960) draws our attention to the ways in which education in any society is an effort to structure perceptions in ways relevant to a particular cultural universe. He points to the internal processes of exclusion, raising the question of the apportionment of the contents of a culture among its members (1960:289). The education system in capitalist societies produces different outcomes by parcelling out different 'knowledges' through exclusion, streaming and other selection techniques. Connell and associates refer to the ways through which the school became, in the postwar decades, a 'sorter and sifter' for the labour market, through a variety of credentialling mechanisms (1982: 197). But the point Henry is making, through cross-cultural comparison, is that we must not look only to the education system for this process. Since the family, too, is involved in 'educating', we must take account of processes inside the family where knowledge is parcelled out on the basis of gender. *Making the Difference* provides us with some excellent examples, although the authors used these examples to demonstrate another point, to which I will return.

The book documents the fragile nature of the hegemonic curriculum:

> [Its effect] . . . is not to *obliterate* ideas and practices which grow out of working-class needs and experiences. It is to disorganise and fragment them; and at the same time it produces resistance to the imposition of academic curriculum. In so doing it is both part and paradigm of the operation of class hegemony in Australian life. (1982:126)

Historically the reform of the curriculum has been in response to working-class demands, yet was achieved on very restricted and conservative conditions, with deeply divisive consequences for working-class families (1982:171). Similarly, the ideology of equal opportunity and the rearrangement of comprehensive education along lines conducive to it, has reinforced a 'distinctive and disempowering tendency in working-class culture'; it is a formula which expresses 'the reconciliation of a genuinely radical and popular demand for more, and empowering, education, with a stratified and competitive social order and the interests which are dominant within it' (1982:196–97). There is no evidence presented in this book that the resolution of conflicting strategies has been on anything but conservative grounds. Again, we have to ask why, and *Making the Difference* provides us with much explanatory material.

The material in the book shows that relationships 'have developed in ways that give different social groups radically different capacities to fashion educational arrangements that are favourable to them' (1982: 190). Further, these different capacities are organised in fundamentally different ways; ruling-class families simply have more options and have professional, powerful 'agents' to ensure the options remain open. The work of school principals in this account demonstrates the different capacities of different actors in fairly precise resource terms, in the sense of strategy options available through the manipulation of the 'space' that market mechanisms provide (1982:137, 155–56).

The different capacities of working-class and ruling-class families are documented in the book through the analysis of the different relationships between the families and their schools. Yet another part of the explanation, referred to earlier in the discussion of the hegemonic curriculum, lies in working-class people's active embracing of this curriculum and their marginalising their own skills and knowledge. As Bourdieu notes.

> social categories disadvantaged by the symbolic order ... cannot but recognise the legitimacy of the dominant classifications in the very fact that their only chance of neutralising those of its effects most damaging to their own interests lies in submitting to them in order to make use of them (1977:164-65).

The account of working-class families' relationships to the education system in *Making the Difference* reveals this strategy, and the praxis traps it leads to. This strategy, in itself, creates and is an expression of a certain ambivalence:

> There are few working-class people who swallow the ideology of 'brains' holus-bolus, yet there are fewer still who reject it completely ... The protests of working-class parents against the abstractness and uselessness of much of the school's knowledge are accompanied by embarrassment, even shame, at being 'uneducated', at not having what the school has. (1982:126)

The working-class school is more than a cultural institution; it is 'a massive intervention by the State into working-class lives' (1982:166), an intervention which 'splits and layers working-class consciousness. The things that working-class people confidently and securely know are pushed aside or devalued as not being proper, socially-recognized knowledge' (1982:169). Of course, knowledge does not exist in two parts, as working-class and ruling-class knowledge; it is produced in a social context and becomes organised and applied in particular ways. The interesting thing about the production of knowledge, its organisation and application, is that on the one hand some kinds of knowledge are more highly valued than others, and on the other the knowledge prized within the working class (relating to the competencies developed on the job) are being organised out of, or being rendered marginal to, the labour process.

But the 'formal' curriculum is as strongly gender-based as it is class-based. Much of the labour referred to in this book, through which particular skills and competencies have developed, has been *masculine* labour. It is sons and fathers struggling over definitions of valuable work and dealing with the tensions developed from their different assessments of the labour market that this book highlights (e.g., 1982: 40). It reflects the devaluation of women's work, inside and outside the labour market.

Working-class women's skills are used in the labour market but are devalued there precisely because they are viewed as the natural attributes of women. In other words, the household, the place in which these skills are acquired, whether transmitted by other women or developed in the course of childrearing, is not regarded as a training place worthy of acknowledgement. The pay for such work in the labour market reflects this devaluation of women's informal training grounds. The analysis in *Making the Difference* does not address the relevance of this and related issues, which means that the subsequent proposals for political action are insufficient for dealing with class-related gender inequality. For instance, the discussion of the pride that people take in their skills, the importance of practical knowledge learnt on the job, renders invisible both the skills developed by women at home and the possibility that, with or without the researchers' prodding, this fact too could have been raised as an issue. It is not irrelevant to current strategies being developed by female unionists in relation to pay rates, and in relation to definitions of 'appropriate experience' for jobs and promotion.

Here, the importance of the working-class school as a state intervention has to be tied up with the analysis of the state's activity in the organisation of domestic life, discussed earlier in this chapter. To separate them is to assume a compartmentalisation of social institutions, again along class–gender lines. The intervention is just as much directed at family life as it is at the labour market. In whose interests? We cannot make sense of these interventions in isolation from what is happening within elite schools, and how strategies are developed there, to what ends. The interests of, for instance, the powerful fathers and their network activities affect the organisation of state education for the working class.

What is in demand by the ruling-class families' places of employment? Mr Walker's world of high-powered business competition requires 'a particular kind of *masculinity:* motivated to compete, strong in the sense of one's own abilities, able to dominate others and to face down opponents in situations of conflict' (1982:73). We need to look, too, at a particular aspect of the hidden curriculum, the gender dimensions of the organisation of schooling in relation to the family.

Although one of the major themes of *Making the Difference* is the mediating by parents that occurs between family and school, the authors do not consider adequately the important difference between the relationships of mothers and fathers to the school.

I have already commented on the tendency to distinguish functions of institutions on the basis of their formal charter and how this obscures the important informal interaction between institutions. This mediating process is one to which *Making the Difference* devotes a great deal of attention. But only with gender centrally in mind can we see that the mediating between the school and the family is not the same for mothers and fathers. In our society childcare is defined as the concern of the family, and education is defined as a teaching process which ends in the middle of the afternoon. This is a false separation. The mother, not the family, is expected to carry out the childcare functions as well as to translate the meaning of education (as carried out within the school) to the small child. It is quite incorrect to imply, as does *Making the Difference,* that the roles of fathers and mothers are similar in this respect, or that if there are differences, (1982:52) they are not central to the analysis.

The structuring of the school day *assumes* a social/sexual division of labour within the family, one which leaves a parent relatively free from paid labour during the day. In fact, the running of the school is predicated on the assumption that *mothers* are available for tuckshops, meetings, fundraising, cake stalls, concerts, displays, parades and auxiliary teaching in, for example, music and physical education. Infant school parents' associations, commonly known as 'Mothers' Clubs', typically meet during the day, so that fathers are on the whole precluded because of work commitments, as well as through ideas about the responsibilities of mothers.

In this and other ways, the structure of the school day inhibits dramatic changes in family-work relationships. For instance, it is not only the lack of childcare facilities at a preschool level which keeps many married women from participation in the paid workforce. A further inhibiting factor is the requirement to prepare children for school in the morning and be at home to receive them at the end of the school day. This illustrates the need to analyse the family-school complex not simply in a temporal family-school sequence. There is a school-family sequence at another level too: mothers play an enormous part in interpreting the school to the child (a need more frequently acted upon than that of interpreting the child to the school).

The importance of this cannot be overestimated. The idea of discontinuities in education is commonly referred to (Henry, 1960; Bernstein, 1975). In our society we have, on the one hand, an ideology of permissive and tolerant child-centred rearing and, on the other, an education system which confronts a 5-year-old with uniforms, discipline, a day divided into 'periods' within which different categories of 'knowledge' are taught (and taught under circumstances quite unrelated to the application of that knowledge), bells, signals and specific times to drink, eat and go to the toilet, and a host of other regulatory rituals. The work-school–family connection has been overestimated in the literature on education at the expense of the school–family connection and the enormous investment in schooling expected of mothers, the unpaid work they do in relation to it and the effects of this on their labour market participation. This poses very real dilemmas for women, although it partly explains the numbers of women in part-time employment. The effect of the education system on the woman in the family needs to be given as much attention in terms of the pressure towards maintaining the 'ideal' familial form as has been given to the 'long shadow of work'.

In *Making the Difference*, the authors' commitment to the possibility of social transformation leads them to question the apparent functionalism of social reproduction theory. Could it be, though, that the reproduction of patterns of inequality are directly tied to the greater capacity of some actors than others to defend and protect their interests? This is not to suggest that they will always be successful in so doing, but it is to suggest that political strategies for change need to be more far-reaching than those suggested in *Making the Difference*, There are many examples, some commented on in this book, of working-class attempts to challenge prevailing views of knowledge, skill and experience, in order to affect the hierarchical ordering of workplaces and the decision-making processes about products and profits. But institutional arrangements (including worker organisations, apparently well suited to the expression and support of collective interests) preclude them from shifting the power base underlying prevailing definitions of the situation. One reason to be lacking in confidence as workers, parents or women is that there are no institutionalised channels for expressing one's personal or collective evaluations of such things, and neither are there institutional arrangements to support, promote and legitimise such views. The negotiation and construction of options, so ably documented in this book, is done from different vantage points and some are more powerful than others.

It is not the case, as Connell and associates argue, that reproduction theorists view the education system as merely reproducing class and gender inequalities, that it investigates the ways in which people are successfully kept in their 'class' and 'gender' places. Reproduction of class and gender inequalities is not 'effortless'. It would appear that the insights which Connell and associates develop about the power relations between groups, and the activities in which they are involved to maintain or change these power relations, provide ample evidence of the obstacles facing working-class people or women intent on the transformation of gender and class inequalities through the education system.

The inadequacy of their account relates in part to their romanticising of the working class, although they are aware of the dangers of doing this (1982:69). They attribute to working-class people more power than their evidence permits, imputing too much freedom to act, or to 'win' in the contests constantly being waged. In addition, they avoid grappling with the overwhelming evidence that the intersection of class and gender, in which they 'abrade, inflame, amplify, twist, negate, dampen and complicate each other' (1982:182) in practice serves to weaken the positions of both the working class and women.

The central problem with *Making the Difference* is that the authors, committed as they are to the active quest for transformation, avoid dealing with the fundamental structural bases of the 'praxis traps' to which they refer. They say, for instance, that 'privileges are not always passed on and under-privilege is not always perpetuated' (1982:188). Yet the evidence presented from case histories supports their comment that 'even where there is a clear goal . . . the means are not automatically at hand' (1982:142), that people are actively constructing 'what they have become and are becoming' (1982:77) under 'terrible constraints', that class–gender interaction overwhelmingly leads to fragmentation, not to strength. The ideology of bi-partisanship, consensus and pragmatism on the part of social democratic political parties has resulted in a set of priorities within which gender inequality is simply too 'expensive' to deal with. Current emphasis in education is on the provision of opportunities for young people—in a context of high unemployment—and in retaining young people at school, at the expense of redressing the unequal access women have had to education in the past, so that mature-age students, mostly women, are being discouraged from participating in higher education. The balance shifts, the social 'problems' change in importance, but while women's political activity is fragmented by class concerns, and while working-class activity is partly a protection of masculine privilege, the situation has to be assessed in less optimistic terms than these authors suggest.

Conclusions

From Engels on, the association of males with public life and females with private life has led to the supposition that, if women were in paid employment, their subordination would be undermined. This line of thought has been modified by feminists, with the acknowledgement of both the 'dual burden' and the systematic discrimination against women within the labour process.

The effects of women's subordination can clearly be seen within the process of capitalist production. The content and organisation of work is a product of class 'structuration' and of gender relationships. The subordination of women, then, cannot be understood simply in terms of the immediate requirements of capitalism. The positions of all women, married and unmarried, mothers and childless, working-class and 'middle-class', are outcomes of an active patriarchal ideology which is no mere echo of market forces. The manifestations of this ideology vary: through time, in accordance with changes in the demand for labour, and from level to level of the class structure in correspondence with varying definitions of 'masculinity' which are the inseparable counterpart of the construction of 'femininity'. These definitions, there is evidence to suggest, are in large part a reflection of the work expectations and experiences of males, which thus become yet another factor to be weighed in any account of the subordination of women.

The connection between women's paid and unpaid work is being increasingly theorised and empirically investigated in contrast to the earlier concern with women as reproducers of labour power within a domestic domain. But we have seen, in the discussions of the state and the education system, that it is impossible to discuss domestic labour without reference to state policies. The law defines and enforces the obligations between spouses and between parents and children. The welfare services effectively penalise any arrangement which violates the criteria by which families are defined. Through the education system, the state also contributes significantly to the perpetuation not only of the class structure but of the social/sexual division of labour. The further analysis proceeds, the more evident it becomes that the institutions and processes contributing to female subordination do so as part of a general process of social reproduction by which state activity contributes to and legitimises capital accumulation.

The radical-feminist homogenisation of 'femininity', and the associated quest for an explanation of women's subordination through a supposedly universal male appropriation of the cultural sphere, gives little in the way of political leverage for change. Besides, 'middle-class'

women are, as women, subordinated in general to the men with whom
they live and work, but as members of the 'middle class' they enjoy
material and social advantages over both male and female members of
the working class. Working-class women, on the other hand, bear the
dual burden of their subordinate gender and class identities. In the
family, as wives and mothers, they are the principal reproducers of the
labour power from which capitalism extracts its surplus, for which
services they receive no payment. In addition, many of them, even
mothers with children, are in paid employment, which permits the
direct extraction of surplus value, while the wages they earn serve to
meet family needs—created in increasing number by capitalism itself—
for which the income of the male 'breadwinner' is insufficient.

It is not childbearing, physical weakness, or any other presumed biologically determined differences that are the basis of women's subordination within capitalist societies. It is the social allocation to
women of responsibilities for children. The obstacles to changing this
connection lie within the capitalist system of production, the vicious
circle of sex-segregated work and the division of labour within the
household.

It is ethnocentric and illogical to assume that because women produce children they (the mothers) are necessarily the childcarers. In
many societies it is not the mothers who take on this role day to day. It
is frequently taken by other members of the community—people who
would not otherwise be productively employed, including older siblings.
The fact that women produce babies bears no relation to female subordination unless, through socially constructed patterns, it precludes
them from access to strategic resources. It certainly does that in capitalist societies.

It would appear from our ethnographic material that in systems
where women are not subordinate to men, they are defined not *in relation* to men, but directly in relation to economic, political and ritual
practices and the power embedded in those practices. An additional
mediating link is required if the construction of assymetrical male-
female relations, based on power, is to appear 'natural'. Within capitalism, it is the reproduction of masculinity and femininity, defined in
relation to each other and materialised in a social/sexual division of
labour, that is important to female subordination.

We have to understand the full impact of the division of men from
children and organise policy recommendations and political activity
around that knowledge. If men had taken part in childcaring and unpaid work as women do now, a transformation of the capitalist mode of

production would necessarily have taken place already.

Without relationships between men and children ever being institutionalised, assumptions about 'motherhood' as against 'adult care' are not overcome. The dichotomy of innate and learned behaviour, and the argument that men must 'learn attachment behaviour' (Tiger and Shepher, 1977; Rossi, 1977) with children, and that it is a 'natural' response on the part of females, are empiricist assertions using data which are already selective—they are based on observations in societies where men do not have the opportunity to deal intimately with infants from the earliest stages of their lives.

A fully adequate theory of socialisation would consider not only the content of the process but, at the least, by whom it is carried out. In these terms, the fact that women predominantly care for infants and children, within the family and within infant and primary schools, must be considered part of the educational program to which children are subjected: in this way women as nurturers and men as remote from children are built into the children's conceptions of their world. Childcare is not an activity separate from the social/sexual division of labour, nor from educational processes, but an integral part of them.

It is worth drawing attention, again, to the ways these processes of attachment and exclusion have implications for the construction of gender, manifested in 'masculinity' and 'femininity' in their different forms. Rather than an inherent tendency, or even something that has been determined for us by the age of five or so, gender is empirically re-created through our experiences, including our experiences of paid and unpaid work.

A program to eliminate gender inequalities would profoundly affect capitalist social relations, involving a radical restructuring of the economy. In a society where married women are an integral part of the paid labour force, the assumption is made that paid work can be performed without heed to childcare. The school day and school holidays bear no relation to adults' hours of employment, and childcare facilities are not generally available. Governments have, at times, acknowledged this problem but have done little to redress the situation.

Equal pay legislation, anti-discrimination laws and programs of affirmative action, although significant in themselves, will not secure equal employment opportunities for women. They are limited in their effectiveness. One of the main reasons lies in the segmentation processes of the labour market. Genuine equal pay is difficult to legislate. There are few jobs which are truly integrated by sex so that 'comparisons between men and women who hold the same kind of job are necessarily limited to an extremely small portion of the labour force' (Stevenson, 1975:224). Moreover, the value attached to different types of work relates to ideas about worth. These ideas result from the combined effects of 'market value', the attribution to women of natural ability as against abilities resulting from training and is anyway an outcome of bargaining between unions and management, bargains based on previous relativities and determinations and which reflect protectionist strategies of categories of workers (see chapters 3 and 4).

As well, job categories have constantly been redefined within organisations, so as to avoid the implications of equal pay legislation. All of the legislated programs directed to equal employment opportunity, moreover, have drawn attention away from the development of policies around the idea that men have responsibilities for childcare and domestic work. Taxation policy, wages policy and social security policy would all need to change to be in line with the initiatives regarding women and employment, so as to restructure not only women's relationship to the labour market but men's relationship to childcare and domestic work.

Feminist theory has begun to develop, however implicitly, an understanding of the dialectical relationship between 'structures' and people, a problem to which much social theory is addressed. The active agency of women which has been discussed in relation to the ethnographic literature is an indication of where future research can go. We need specific studies of counter or muted female ideologies: active though often covert or silent responses to particular circumstances and embodied in social practices.[9]

The feminist movement is a visible manifestation of the fact that women are not simply passive recipients of a dominant ideology which imposes on them a definition of their place. There are, moreover, less visible responses by women to the contradictions in their lives, which careful empirical research could uncover.

Theories of women's subordination are contributions to a more general theory of social reproduction. They refer to the specific content and manifestation of socially constructed relationships between the sexes. This construction involves the exercise of power, which can be located in economic, political, legal and symbolic practices. It is the concern of feminist theory to reveal the nature of that power and of its interaction to the responses it provokes. But this should be more than a feminist concern. The problems and insights which feminist theory has brought to light have now to be assimilated by social theory in general.

Notes

CHAPTER 1

1 To be referred to as *Origin of the Family*
2 For the inadequacies of the Rev. John Roscoe's account, see Mair (1965:xiii), who concludes: 'It is most inadequate at those points at which the student of economic contact most requires accurate and detailed information—in such questions as the system of economic co-operation, or of land tenure, or the relations between people and chiefs.' There is a mass of literature on the Buganda, much of which was published before Sacks' account. See, for instance, Apter (1961); Fallers (ed.) (1964). See also Low (1971)
3 See Tiftany, 1978, for a recent and comprehensive overview of the anthropology of women. She rejects the argument that women have been generally subordinate to men
4 This is similar to the conception of historical reconstruction outlined by Althusser and Balibar, 1975. See also Godelier in an interview with Lévi-Strauss (Lévi-Strauss, Angé and Godelier, 1976)
5 I am intrigued by Aaby's obvious concern to use non-sexist language, when the object of his discussion can only be females!
6 The works of Young and Willmott, 1957, and Bott, 1957, which trace women's close links with their kinswomen, are drawn upon by Mitchell
7 This article was first published in 1971 and later in Skolnick and Skolnick (1974) and Reiter (ed.) (1975). Two other articles by Gough, 'Women in evolution' (n.d.) and 'An anthropologist looks at Engels' (1972) are concerned with the same theme. These are shorter and were not as readily available as the article discussed in this chapter. The latter article was written especially for the book edited by Glazer-Malbin and Waehrer (1972). Its importance lies, I think, in the ways Gough corrects some of the details of Engels' chronology of events. She does this through more recent archaeological discoveries. The undated article appears to have been written after the other two. Here Gough is more concerned with the contemporary connection between women's oppression and class, as well as 'war, imperialism, racism, genocide and man-made poverty' (n.d.: 11)
8 For the historically variable content of the relationships between parents and children, and mothers and infants, see, for example, Ariès (1973); Shorter (1976); and de Mause (ed.) (1976)

CHAPTER 2

1 For example, Edholm, Harris and Young (1977); Mackintosh (1977); Molyneux (1977); O'Laughlin (1977)
2 Published in English by Cambridge University Press (1981)
3 See R. Morgan (ed.) (1970). Sacks's doctoral dissertation (1971) was based on material from the four societies discussed in her 1974 article. See also Sacks (1976)
4 The original (1974) version was revised for publication in Reiter (ed.) (1975)
5 The terms 'emic' and 'etic' were introduced into social anthropology by Harris (1968). See also Leacock (1972); Friedl (1975); and O'Laughlin (1975)
6 An interesting theoretical account of women's *apparent* passivity is provided by E. Ardener (1975), and his ideas have informed empirical work. See S. Ardener (ed.) (1975). When Ardener refers to the 'muted' character of women's communication, he emphasises that this is not 'some condition of linguistic silence', but that it occurs because 'it does not form part of the dominant communicative system of the society' (1975:22). He applies this idea to other dominated groups, including classes. For a criticism of his work, see Mathieu (1978)
7 According to Mair's account, this is not the case. The cultivation of Simsim required a cooperative work group of women (Mair, 1965:123, 125)

CHAPTER 3

1 The only article in this collection which does not rely on such a conceptualisation is Bridget O'Laughlin's (1974). She rejects any universal opposition of this kind
2 See Willis (1977:153) for white working-class males' attitudes towards West Indians and Asians, and how the latter's jobs are defined as 'dirty' as against their own as 'masculine'
3 See also Komarovsky (1964) and my discussion of research techniques in this chapter
4 See my bibliography for a list of the publications in the *Affluent Worker* series. See also Goldthorpe (1966); Goldthorpe and Lockwood (1963); Lockwood (1958, 1960, 1975)
5 'Affluent' means manual workers with 'personal and family incomes comparable to those of many white-collar employees, minor professionals and smaller independents' (Goldthorpe et al., 1969:32)
6 As contrasted with traditional and deferential workers. These distinctions will not concern us here
7 Compare this with Sennett's and Cobb's explanation of this reluctance (1973:147-50). See also Willis (1977:167-68)

8 The research was carried out in Luton, in south-west Bedfordshire.
   There was a high proportion of migrants to Luton, which had rapidly
   expanded industrially in the postwar years. The workers interviewed were employed in three major manufacturing plants
9 Sennett said this in an interview with me on *Broadband*, ABC
   Radio, 4 April 1978. See chapter 4, though, for variations in patterns within the working class
10 See also Seeley et al. (1963); Cooper (1971); Laing (1972) and
   Sennett and Cobb (1973) for children's experiences and responses

CHAPTER 4

1 For excellent descriptive and historical accounts of domestic labour
   under capitalism, see Rowbotham (1973) and Oakley (1974a,
   1974b)
2 This article was produced as a pamphlet by the Female Revolutionary Educational School, Cambridge, Mass.; it was reproduced by
   the Women's Liberation Workshop, London, and by the Women's
   Liberation Movement, Sydney, Australia
3 See Fee's criticism of arguments which rest on the assumption that
   'strategic implications could be deduced from how one defined one's
   problem' (1976:7)
4 This debate was carried out mainly within the pages of the *Bulletin
   of the Conference of Socialist Economists.* However, a few were
   not. The contours of this debate are very much influenced by who
   reads which journal. For instance, Seccombe refers to publications
   in the *New Left Review* but not to contributions in the *CSEB.*
   Howell's (1975) contribution to this wider argument as well as to
   housework and its relation to capital has been referred to only in
   the next issue of *Revolutionary Communist* after his article was
   published (Adamson et al., 1976). These are the main contributions to this wider discussion that was proceeding at the time:
   Gough, I. (1972, 1973); Harrison (1973a, 1973b); Gough and
   Harrison (1975); Fine (1973); Bullock (1973, 1974); Howell
   (1975)
5 Greer makes a similar point: 'The weapon that I suggest is that
   most honoured of the proletariat, withdrawal of labour. Nevertheless . . . I do not find the factory the real heart of civilisation or the
   re-entry of women into industry as the necessary condition of liberation' (1971:22)
6 See, for instance, Beresford (1974), who says of the domestic
   mode of production argument, 'The inspiration for this develop-

ment has clearly come from the possibilities offered in two articles by Dalla Costa and Margaret Benston from Italy and Canada' (1974:44)

7 Vort-Ronald's paper 'Women and Class' was delivered at the National Women's Conference on Feminism and Socialism, October, 1974, Melbourne, Australia. It was published in the Papers of the Conference. It was also published as an article in *Refractory Girl*, No. 7, 20–6 (1974). This is a major publication of the feminist movement in Australia

8 A shortened version of a paper delivered to The Conference of Marxist Scholars at the University of Adelaide, 14 September, (1974a). For the list of authors, see the bibliography

9 Gardiner et al. (1975) and Brennan (1977) also make it clear that they concentrate on the 'political economy' aspect of women's domestic work. But their criticisms of Seccombe do not recognise that he was doing likewise

10 Figures from the 1971 General Household Census, Great Britain, indicate that in 1971, in unskilled manual-worker families, 55.6 per cent owned a refrigerator, 60.2 per cent a washing machine and 76.7 per cent a vacuum cleaner (Adamson et al., 1976:25)

11 The authors deliberately refer to domestic work as 'toil' and not as 'labour'. A similar distinction is accepted by Curthoys and Barbalet (1976). They say that 'Engels noted that "the English language has two different expressions ... in the simple labour process, the process of producing use-values, it is *work*, in the process of creating value, it is *labour*, taking the term in its strict economic sense" ' (Curthoys and Barbalet, 1976:4). Strictly, they are right. But Campioni (1976a) might have a point when she says that this further stresses the economy/family distinction and obscures the necessary aspect of the work. Too much concern with precision of terminology may actually hinder clear presentation of the main points of arguments

12 See, for instance, Power (1978); Adamson et al. (1976); *Women and Labour Conference Papers*, Conference held at Macquarie University, Sydney, May 1978, published by the Convenors, School of History, Philosophy and Politics, Macquarie University, Sydney

13 Compare, for example, Blood and Wolfe (1960); Szymanski (1976)

14 See, for instance, Dalla Costa (1973:32); Humphries (1976:108); James (1974:17); Ryan and Rowse (1975:17,30). Gardiner (1975) and Wilson (1977), for Great Britain, and Brennan (1977), for Australia, point out the more complex ways the union movement has responded to women's demands over time, and how demands in the interests of the working class as a whole may at different times conflict with women's needs for employment

15 See Sennett (1970); Sennett and Cobb (1973); Goldthorpe et al.,

1969. No equivalent research has been carried out in Australia, although the data that are available are suggestive. Married men's 'multiple job-holding' and extent of overtime reported in the official statistics are undoubtedly understated. The statistics, however, indicate that working overtime is very common, and having more than one (official) job is not uncommon. The extent to which this occurs in families where the wife–mother does not work in paid employment needs to be researched, preferably not by Government officials, for the full extent of its occurrence to come to light. Several factors make the hypothesis plausible: for instance, married women's participation in the workforce is related in complex ways to ethnic origin and education, among other things. Education has little impact on migrant women's participation, but significantly affects Australian-born women's participation. The more education they have had the more likely they are to be in the paid workforce. Since those women with fewer years of education are likely to be married to men at a similar level of education, one problem remains unanswered: how the man's (single) wage supports a full-time housewife and dependants. For the patterns of employment of married women, Australian-born, and migrant, see *The Role of Women in the Economy*, Women's Bureau, Department of Labour (1974), and *'But I wouldn't want my wife to work here...'*, Research Report for International Women's Year, Centre for Urban Research and Action (1975). For overtime and multiple job-holding *official* statistics, see Australian Bureau of Statistics *Earnings in Hours of Employees, Distribution and Composition; Multiple Job-holding*

CHAPTER 5

1 This does not have the same meaning as 'false consciousness'
2 Elsewhere Freud explains 'psychical intensity' to mean 'the degree of interest of an idea' (1976:415)
3 See Ch. 1 of *The Elementary Structures of Kinship* (1969). See also Ch. 29, part 4, where Lévi-Strauss addresses Freud's *Totem and Taboo*. But see also Lévi-Strauss' other works. In particular, see *Structural Anthropology* (1963)
4 For an outline of Lacan's use of these concepts see Gross (1976)
5 For a discussion of the structuralism of Marxist theorists see Makarius (1974), Veltmeyer (1974–75), among others
6 More recently, the argument that historical materialism and psychoanalysis constitute sciences (as distinct from ideological theories), or that a clear distinction can be made between scientific and ideological discourses, has been abandoned. Currently the notion of

'theoretical discourses' is used to overcome what appears to be a false dichotomy. At the time, though, it led to this insistence on the elimination of 'ideology' from the sciences of historical materialism and psychoanalysis. See Bullen (1976), who points to the confusion of two things in much of this literature: the sciences and the objects of the sciences

CHAPTER 6

1 See also Land, 1976, for a detailed examination of the Beveridge Report and its assumptions about, and implications for, women
2 For detailed examinations of the historical changes in these relationships, see Land, 1976; Land and Parker, 1978 for Britain; and Brennan, 1977; Edwards, 1979a, 1979b, 1980a, 1980c for Australia
3 I am indebted not only to the work of Meredith Edwards, but to many personal communications with her. This section by no means exhausts the policy implications of her analysis. It is intended to suggest the directions that need to be pursued
4 An exception to this is provided by David, 1978. For an extensive bibliography of feminist and other approaches to the education system, see Torch (ed.), 1976
5 For a selection of this literature, see Brown (ed.), 1973; Bernstein, 1971, 1975; Young (ed.), 1971; Bowles, Gintis and Meyer, 1975; Bourdieu and Passeron, 1977
6 For example, Bowles, Gintis and Meyer, 1974–75, 1975, 1975–76; Sennett and Cobb, 1973; Poulantzas, 1975; Habermas, 1976. In the Australian context: Catley and McFarlane, 1974; Game and Pringle, 1977. The conceptualisations are not necessarily the same. The point they have in common, though, is that a shift has occurred to a *narrower* definition of what makes one eligible for opportunities in the first place, and the notion of intelligence is playing a stronger part
7 See Sharp and Green, 1975, for descriptions of this process within the classroom. See also Sennett and Cobb, 1973, for observations as well as for personal accounts of how this operated within the workplace
8 See Althusser 1971 (1978b) and Poulantzas, 1975. Miliband 1969 (1973a) was also influential. For the debates between Miliband and Poulantzas, see Miliband, 1972, 1973b and Poulantzas, 1972, 1976. Among others, Laclau, 1975 comments on this debate
9 The anthropological literature is rich in this respect. See, for instance, Strathern, 1972; E Ardener, 1975, S. Ardener, (ed.), 1975. See also Hobson, 1978; McRobbie, 1978

Bibliography

Aaby, Peter (1977) 'Engels and women' *Critique of Anthropology* 3, 9 and 10, pp. 25-53

Adamson, Olivia, Carol Brown, Judith Harrison and Judy Price (1976) 'Women's oppression under capitalism' *Revolutionary Communist* 5, pp. 2-48

Adlam, Diana and Angie Salfield (1978) 'A matter of language: Coward and Ellis' *Language and Materialism' Ideology and Consciousness* 3, pp. 95-111

Allen, S., L. Sanders and J. Wallis (eds) (1974) *Conditions of Illusion* Leeds: Feminist Books Ltd

Altbach, Edith (ed.) (1971) *From Feminism to Liberation* Cambridge, Mass: Schenkman Publishing

Althusser, Louis (1969) *For Marx* transl. Ben Brewster, Harmondsworth, Middlesex: Penguin Books

— ((1971) 1978a) *Lenin and Philosophy and Other Essays* transl. Ben Brewster, New York: Monthly Review Press

— ((1971) 1978b) 'Ideology and ideological state apparatuses' in Althusser *Lenin and Philosophy and Other Essays* pp. 127-86

— ((1971) 1978c) 'Freud and Lacan' in Althusser *Lenin and Philosophy and Other Essays* pp. 189-219

Althusser, Louis and Etienne Balibar ((1970) 1975) *Reading Capital* transl. Ben Brewster, London: New Left Books

Anderson, Michael (ed.) (1971) *Sociology of the Family* Harmondsworth, Middlesex: Penguin Books

Anderson, Perry (1965) 'Origins of the present crisis' in Anderson and Blackburn (eds) *Towards Socialism* pp. 11-52

Anderson, Perry and Robin Blackburn (eds) (1965) *Towards Socialism* London: The Fontana Library

Apter, David E. (1961) *The Political Kingdom in Uganda* Princeton, New Jersey: Princeton University Press

Ardener, Edwin ((1972) 1975) 'Belief and the problem of women' in Ardener (ed.) *Perceiving Women* pp. 1-17

Ardener, Shirley (ed.) (1975) *Perceiving Women* London: Malaby Press

Ardrey, Robert (1961) *African Genesis* New York: Delta Books

— (1966) *The Territorial Imperative* New York: Delta Books

Ariès, Philippe ((1960) 1973) *Centuries of childhood* Harmondsworth, Middlesex: Penguin Books

Australian Bureau of Statistics (1977a) *Earnings in Hours of Employees, Distribution and Composition* May

— (1977b) *Multiple Jobholding August*

— (1977c) *Persons not in the Labour Force* May

— (1978) *Family, Information Paper* May

— (1980) *The Labour Force* September

Bachofen, Johann Jakob ((1861) 1967) 'Mother Right' in *Myth, Religion and Mother Right* transl. Ralph Manheim, Princeton: Princeton University Press

Bakan, David (1972) 'Psychology can now kick the science habit' *Psychology Today* 5, 10, pp. 26, 28, 86–88

Baldock, Cora V. and Bettina Cass (eds) (1983) *Women, Social Welfare and the State* Sydney: George Allen and Unwin

Barker, Diana Leonard and Sheila Allen (eds) (1976a) *Sexual Divisions and Society: Process and Change* London: Tavistock Publications

— (1976b) *Dependence and Exploitation in Work and Marriage* London: Longman

Barrett, Michelle (1980) *Women's Oppression Today: Problems in Marxist Feminist Analysis* London: Verso

Bart, Pauline B. (1971) 'Sexism and social science: from the gilded cage to the iron cage, or, the perils of Pauline' *Journal of Marriage and the Family* 33, 4, pp. 734–45

Beechey, Veronica (1977) 'Some notes on female wage labour in capitalist production' *Capital and Class* 3, Autumn, pp. 45–66

— (1978) 'Women and production: a critical analysis of some sociological theories of women's work' in Kuhn and Wolpe *Feminism and Materialism*

— (1979) 'On Patriarchy' *Feminist Review* 3, pp. 66–82

Beidelman, T.O. (ed.) ((1971) 1973) *The Translation of Culture* London: Tavistock Publications

Benedict, Ruth ((1935) 1961) *Patterns of Culture* London: Routledge and Kegan Paul

Benston, Margaret (1969) 'The political economy of women' *Monthly Review* 21, 4, pp. 13–27

Beresford, Melanie (1974) 'The domestic mode of production revisited' *Refractory Girl* 6, pp. 44–48

Bernard, Jessie ((1972) 1976) *The Future of Marriage* Harmondsworth, Middlesex: Penguin Books

Bernstein, Basil (1971) *Class, Codes and Control* vol. 1, *Theoretical Studies towards a Sociology of Language* London: Routledge and Kegan Paul

— (1975) *Class, Codes and Control* vol. 3, *Towards a Theory of Educational Transmissions* London: Routledge and Kegan Paul

Beveridge, W. (1942) 'Social Insurance and Allied Services' (the Beveridge Report) Cmnd 6404, London: HMSO

Blackburn, Robin (ed.) (1972) *Ideology in Social Science* Glasgow: Fontana Books

Blackburn, Robin and Michael Mann (1975) 'Ideology in the non-skilled working class' in Martin Bulmer (ed.) *Working Class Images of Society* London: Routledge and Kegan Paul

Bland, Lucy, Rachel Harrison, Frank Mort and Christine Weedon (1978) 'Relations of reproduction: approaches through anthropology' in Women's Studies Group *Women Take Issue*

Bland, Lucy, Trisha McCabe and Frank Mort (1978), Women, ideologies and theories of reproduction, paper presented to the British Sociological Annual Conference, Brighton, England

Blaxall, Martha and Barbara Reagan (eds) (1976) *Women and the Workplace: the implications of occupational segregation* Chicago: University of Chicago Press

Bloch, Maurice (1975) 'Property and the end of affinity' in Maurice Bloch (ed.) *Marxist Analyses and Social Anthropology* London: Malaby Press

Blood, Robert and Donald Wolfe (1960) *Husbands and Wives* Glencoe, Illinois: The Free Press

Bohannan, Laura (1949) 'Dahomean Marriage: A Revaluation' *Africa* 19, pp. 273-87

Bott, Elizabeth (1957) *Family and Social Network* London: Tavistock Publications

Bourdieu, Pierre (1977) *Outline of a Theory of Practice* transl. Richard Nice, Cambridge: Cambridge University Press

Bourdieu, Pierre and Jean-Claude Passeron (1977) *Reproduction in Education, Society and Culture* transl. Richard Nice, London: Sage Publications

Bowles, Samuel, Herbert Gintis and Peter Meyer (1974-75) 'The long shadow of work: education, the family and the reproduction of the social division of labor' *The Insurgent Sociologist* 5, pp. 3-21

— (1975) *Schooling in Capitalist America: Educational Reform and the Contradictions of Economic Life* New York: Basic Books

— (1975-76) 'Education, I.Q. and the legitimation of the social division of labor' *Berkeley Journal of Sociology* 20, pp. 233-64

Brennan, Teresa (1977) 'Women and work' *Journal of Australian Political Economy* October, pp. 34-52

Brennan, Teresa, Mia Campioni and Elizabeth Jacka (1976) 'One step forward, two steps back: a Marxist critique of Juliet Mitchell's *Psychoanalysis and Feminism*' *Working Papers in Sex, Science and Culture* 1, 1, pp. 15-45

Briggs, Jean (1974) 'Eskimo women: makers of men' in Matthiasson (ed.) *Many Sisters*

Brown, Judith (1970) 'Economic organization and the position of women among the Iroquois' *Ethnohistory* 7, pp. 151-67

Brown, Richard (ed.) (1973) *Knowledge, Education, and Cultural Change* London: Tavistock Publications

Bullen, Jane (1976) '"Patriarchy", psychoanalysis and historical materialism' *Working Papers in Sex, Science and Culture* 1, 1, pp. 46-54

Bullock, P. (1973) 'Categories of labour power for capital' *Bulletin of the
Conference of Socialist Economists* Autumn, pp. 82-99

— (1974) 'Defining productive labour for capital' *Bulletin of the Conference of Socialist Economists* Autumn, pp. 1-15

Bulmer, Martin (1975) 'Some problems of research into class imagery' in
Martin Bulmer (ed.) *Working Class Images of Society* London: Routledge and Kegan Paul

Burniston, Steve, Frank Mort and Christine Weedon (1978) 'Psychoanalysis and the cultural acquisition of sexuality and subjectivity'
in Women's Studies Group *Women Take Issue*

Burton, Clare (1979) From the family to social reproduction: the development of feminist theory, PhD thesis, Macquarie University, Sydney

— (1983) Documenting the Power Structure in Academic Institutions,
paper presented to a conference on Equal Opportunity in Tertiary
Institutions, Macquarie University, Sydney, 27-28 September, 1983

Campioni, Mia (1976a) 'Reply to Jean Curthoys' in *Selected Papers from
the first Australian Political Economy Conference* Sydney University: Australian Political Economy Movement

— (1976b) 'Psychoanalysis and Marxist-feminism' *Working Papers in
Sex, Science and Culture* 1, 2, pp. 33-59

Campioni, Mia, Elizabeth Jacka, Paul Patton, Pat Skenridge, Margo
Moore and David Wells (1974a) Opening the floodgates: domestic
labour and capitalist production, paper presented to the Conference of
Marxist Scholars, University of Adelaide, 14 September 1974

— (1974b) 'Opening the floodgates: domestic labour and capitalist production' *Refractory Girl* 7, pp. 10-14

Catley, Robert and Bruce McFarlane (1974) *From Tweedledum to
Tweedledee* Sydney: Australian and New Zealand Book Co.

Centre for Urban Research and Action (1975) 'But I wouldn't want my
wife to work here . . .' *Research Report for International Women's
Year* Fitzroy, Victoria: Centre for Urban Research and Action

Childe, Gordon ((1951) 1963) *Social Evolution* London: Collins, The
Fontana Library

Chodorow, Nancy (1978) *The Reproduction of Mothering: Psychoanalysis and the Sociology of Gender* Berkeley: University of California Press

Cockburn, Cynthia (1981) 'The material of male power' *Feminist Review*
9, pp. 41-58

— (1983) *Brothers: Male Dominance and Technological Change*
London: Pluto Press

Comer, Lee (1974) 'Functions of the family' in Allen, Saunders and
Wallis (eds) *Conditions of Illusion*

Commonwealth Bureau of Census and Statistics (1969) *Child Care* May

Connell, R.W. (1974) 'The causes of educational inequality: further observations' *Australian and New Zealand Journal of Sociology* 10, 3,
pp. 186–89
— (1977) *Ruling Class, Ruling Culture* Cambridge: Cambridge University Press
— (1980a) How should we theorize patriarchy, unpublished paper, Macquarie University, Sydney
— (1980b) On crisis tendencies in patriarchy and capitalism, unpublished
paper, a revised and condensed version of a paper given to the 1979
Conference of Socialist Economists, Leeds
— (1983) *Which Way is Up? Essays on Class, Sex and Culture* Sydney:
George Allen and Unwin
Connell, R.W., D.J. Ashenden, S. Kessler and G.W. Dowsett (1982)
Making the Difference: Schools, Families and Social Division
Sydney: George Allen and Unwin
Connell, R.W. and T.H. Irving (1980) *Class Structure in Australian
History* Melbourne: Longman Cheshire
Cooper, David (1971) *The Death of the Family* London: Allen Lane,
Penguin Books
Coulson, Margaret, Magas Branka and Hilary Wainwright (1975) 'The
housewife and her labour under capitalism' *New Left Review* 89, pp.
59–71
Critique of Anthropology 3, 9 and 10, 1977
Crook, J.H. (1977) 'On the integration of gender strategies in mam-
malian social systems' in Rosenblatt and Komisaruk (eds) *Reproduc-
tive Behaviour and Evolution*
Curthoys, Ann, Susan Eade and Peter Spearritt (eds) (1975) *Women at
Work* Canberra: Australian Society for the Study of Labour History
Curthoys, Ann and J. Barbalet (1976) 'Women: class or class deter-
mined? A Marxist analysis of housework' in *Selected Papers from the
first Australian Political Economy Conference* Sydney University:
Australian Political Economy Movement
Dalla Costa, Mariarosa ((1972) 1973) *The Power of Women and the Sub-
version of the Community* Bristol: Falling Wall Press
David, Miriam E. (1978) 'The family-education couple: towards an
analysis of the William Tyndale dispute' in Littlejohn et al. (eds)
Power and the State
Davidoff, Leonore (1976) 'The rationalization of housework' in Barker
and Allen (eds) *Dependence and Exploitation*
Davis, Elizabeth Gould (1972) *The First Sex* Baltimore, Maryland:
Penguin Books
de Beauvoir, Simone ((1949) 1972) *The Second Sex* transl. and ed. H.M.
Parshley, Harmondsworth, Middlesex: Penguin Books
Deere, Carmen (1976) 'Rural women's subsistence production in the
capitalist periphery' *Review of Radical Political Economics* 8, 1, pp.

9-17

de George, Richard and Fernande de George (eds) (1972) *The Structuralists from Marx to Lévi-Strauss* Garden City, New York: Anchor Books, Doubleday and Co.

Delphy, C. (1971) 'The Main Enemy' in Women's Research and Resources Centre *The Main Enemy*

de Mause, Lloyd (ed.) (1976) *The History of Childhood. The evolution of parent-child relationships as a factor in history* London: Souvenir Press

de Saussure, Ferdinand (1960) *Course in General Linguistics* transl. Wade Baskin, London: Peter Owen

Diggs, Elizabeth (1972) 'What is the women's movement?' *Women: A Journal of Liberation* 2, 4, 10-13

Douglas, M. (1970) *Purity and Danger, An Analysis of Concepts of Pollution and Taboo* Harmondsworth, Middlesex: Penguin Books

Dunbar, Roxanne (1970) 'Female liberation as the basis for social revolution' in Morgan (ed.) *Sisterhood is Powerful*

Duncan, Graeme (ed.) (1978) *Critical Essays in Australian Politics* Melbourne: Edward Arnold

Dunn, Patrick P. (1976) '"That enemy is the baby": childhood in Imperial Russia' in de Mause (ed.) *The History of Childhood*

Edholm, Felicity, Olivia Harris and Kate Young (1977) 'Conceptualising women' *Critique of Anthropology* 3, 9 and 10, pp. 101-130

Edwards, J. (ed.) (1969) *The Family and Change* New York: Alfred A. Knopf Inc.

Edwards, M. (1979a) 'The tax-transfer treatment of married couples' *Australia Quarterly* 51, 2, pp. 46-53

— (1979b) 'Taxation and the family unit: social aspects' in *Taxation and the Family Unit*, proceedings of a seminar convened and published by the Taxation Research and Education Institute, Sydney, pp. 29-39

— (1980a) Social effects of taxation, paper presented to the 46th Australian Institute of Political Science Summer School, January 1980

— (1980b) Financial Arrangements within Families, unpublished study undertaken for the National Women's Advisory Council

— (1980c) 'Social effects of taxation' in John Wilkes (ed.) *The Politics of Taxation* Sydney: Hodder and Stoughton

Edwards, Richard C., Michael Reich and Thomas E. Weisskopf (eds) (1972) *The Capitalist System* Englewood Cliffs, New Jersey: Prentice-Hall Inc.

Edwards, Richard C., Michael Reich and David M. Gordon (eds) (1975) *Labor Market Segmentation* Lexington, Mass: D.C. Heath and Co.

Ehrensaft, Diane (1980) 'When women and men mother' *Socialist Review* 10, 1 (Jan-Feb) pp. 37-73

Eisenstein, Hester (1984) *Contemporary Feminist Thought* London: Unwin Paperbacks

Eisenstein, Zillah (1979) 'Developing a theory of capitalist patriarchy and socialist feminism' in Zillah R. Eisenstein (ed.) *Capitalist Patriarchy and the Case for Socialist Feminism* New York: Monthly Review Press

Engels, Frederick ((1844) 1969) *The Condition of the Working Class in England* London: Panther Books

— ((1880) 1970a) *Socialism: Utopian and Scientific* in Marx and Engels *Selected Works* vol. 3

— (1884) (1970b) *The Origin of the Family, Private Property and the State* in Marx and Engels *Selected Works* vol. 3

Erikson, Erik (1950) *Childhood and Society* New York: W.W. Norton

Evans-Pritchard, E.E. (1945) 'Some aspects of marriage and the family among the Nuer' *Rhodes-Livingstone Papers* no. 11, London: Oxford University Press

— (1951) *Kinship and Marriage among the Nuer* Oxford: Clarendon Press

Fallers, Lloyd (ed.) (1964) *The King's Men: Leadership and Status in Buganda on the Eve of Independence* London: Oxford University Press

Fanon, Franz (1970) *Black Skin White Masks* transl. Charles Lam Markmann, London: Paladin

Fee, Terry (1976) 'Domestic labor: an analysis of housework and its relation to the production process' *Review of Radical Political Economics* 8, 1, pp. 1-8

Figes, Eva ((1970) 1972) *Patriarchal Attitudes* London: Panther Books

Fine, Ben (1973) 'A note on productive and unproductive labour' *Bulletin of the Conference of Socialist Economists* Autumn, pp. 99-102

Firestone, Shulamith ((1970) 1972) *The Dialectic of Sex* London: Paladin

Frankel, Boris (1978) *Marxian Theories of the State: A Critique of Orthodoxy* Arena Monograph Series No. 3, Victoria, Australia: Arena Publications Association

Frankenberg, R. (1966) *Communities in Britain* Harmondsworth, Middlesex: Penguin Books

Fraser, Andrew (1976) 'Legal theory and legal practice' *Arena* (Australia) 44-45, pp. 123-56

Freedman, Marcia (1976) *Segments and Shelters* Montclair: Landmark Studies, Allanheld, Osmun and Co.

Freud, S. ((1940) 1959) *An Outline of Psycho-Analysis* transl. James Strachey, London: The Hogarth Press

— ((1950) 1960) *Totem and Taboo* transl. James Strachey, London: Routledge and Kegan Paul

— ((1901) 1975) *The Psychopathology of Everyday Life* transl. Alan Tyson, Harmondsworth, Middlesex: Pelican Freud Library, vol. 5

— ((1900) 1976) *The Interpretation of Dreams* transl. James Strachey,

Harmondsworth, Middlesex: Pelican Freud Library, vol. 4

Friedan, Betty ((1963) 1965) *The Feminine Mystique* Harmondsworth, Middlesex: Penguin Books

Friedl, Ernestine (1975) *Women and Men. An Anthropologist's View* New York: Holt, Rinehart and Winston

Game, Ann and Pringle, Rosemary (1977) 'The feminist movement, the state and the Labor Party' *Intervention* (Australia) 8, pp. 45-62

— (1978) 'Women and Class in Australia: Feminism and the Labor Government' in Duncan (ed.) *Critical Essays in Australian Politics*

— (1983) *Gender at Work* Sydney: George Allen and Unwin

Gardiner, Jean (1975) 'Women's domestic labour' *New Left Review* 89, pp. 47-58

Gardiner, Jean, Susan Himmelweit and Maureen Mackintosh (1975) 'Women's domestic labour' in *On the Political Economy of Women* CSE Pamphlet no. 2, London: Stage I

Glazer-Malbin, Nona and Helen Y. Waehrer (eds) (1972) *Women in a Man-made World. A socio-economic handbook* New York: Rand McNally and Co.

Godelier, Maurice (1975) 'Modes of production, kinship, and demographic structures' in Bloch (ed.) *Marxist Analyses and Social Anthropology*

Goldthorpe, John H. (1966) 'Attitudes and behaviour of car assembly workers: a deviant case and a theoretical critique' *British Journal of Sociology* 17, 3, pp. 227-44

Goldthorpe, John H. and David Lockwood (1963) 'Affluence and the British class structure' *Sociological Review* 11, 2, pp. 133-63

Goldthorpe, John H., David Lockwood, Frank Bechhofer and Jennifer Platt (1968a) *The Affluent Worker: Political Attitudes and Behaviour* Cambridge: Cambridge University Press

— (1968b) *The Affluent Worker: Industrial Attitudes and Behaviour* Cambridge: Cambridge University Press

— (1969) *The Affluent Worker in the Class Structure* Cambridge: Cambridge University Press

Gough, Ian (1972) 'Productive and unproductive labour in Marx' *New Left Review* 76, pp. 47-72

— (1973) 'On productive and unproductive labour—reply' *Bulletin of the Conference of Socialist Economists* Winter, pp. 68-73

Gough, Ian and John Harrison (1975) 'Unproductive labour and housework again' *Bulletin of the Conference of Socialist Economists* February, pp. 1-7

Gough, Kathleen (n.d.) *Women in Evolution* pamphlet, Toronto: New Hogtown Press

— (1959) 'The Nayars and the definition of marriage' *Journal of the Royal Anthropological Institute* 89, pp. 23-34

— (1968) 'New proposals for anthropologists' *Current Anthropology* 9,

5, pp. 403-7

— (1972) 'An anthropologist looks at Engels' in Glazer-Malbin and Waehrer (eds) *Woman in a Man-made World*

— ((1971) 1973) 'Nuer kinship: a re-examination' in Beidelman (ed.) *The Translation of Culture*

— ((1971) 1975) 'The origins of the family' in Reiter (ed.) *Toward an Anthropology of Women*

Graveson, R.H. and F.R. Crane (eds) (1957) *A Century of Family Law* London: Sweet and Maxwell

Gray, Robert F. and P.H. Gulliver (eds) (1964) *The Family Estate in Africa* London: Routledge and Kegan Paul

Greenwood, Victoria and Jock Young (1976) *Abortion in Demand* London: Pluto Press

Greer, Germaine (1971) *The Female Eunuch* London: Paladin

Gross, Elizabeth (1976) 'Lacan, the Symbolic, the Imaginary and the Real' *Working Papers in Sex, Science and Culture* 1, 2, pp. 12-32

Habermas, J. (1976) *Legitimation Crisis* transl. Thomas McCarthy, London: Heinemann

Hacker, Sally L. (1979) 'Sex stratification, technology and organizational change: a longitudinal case study of AT & T' *Social Problems* 26, 5, pp. 539-57

Harris, Marvin (1968) *The Rise of Anthropological Theory* London: Routledge and Kegan Paul

Harrison, John (1973a) 'Productive and unproductive labour in Marx's political economy' *Bulletin of the Conference of Socialist Economists* pp. 70-82

— (1973b) 'The political economy of housework' *Bulletin of the Conference of Socialist Economists* pp. 35-52

Hartmann, Heidi (1976) 'Capitalism, Patriarchy, and Job Segregation by Sex' in Blaxall and Reagan (eds) *Women and the Workplace*

Henry, Jules (1960) 'A cross-cultural outline of education' *Current Anthropology* 1, 4, pp. 267-305

Herbert, Ralph and Michael Emmison (1977) 'Social contacts amongst suburban housewives' *Australian Journal of Social Issues* 12, 4, pp. 307-315

Hindell, Keith and Madeleine Simms (1968) 'How the abortion lobby worked' *Political Quarterly* 39, 3, pp. 269-82

Hobson, Dorothy (1978) 'Housewives: isolation as oppression' in Women's Studies Group *Women Take Issue*

Hole, Judith and Ellen Levine (1971) *Rebirth of Feminism* New York: Quadrangle Books

Howell, Peter (1975) 'Once again on productive and unproductive labour' *Revolutionary Communist* 3-4, pp. 46-68

Humphries, Jane (1976) 'Women: spacegoats and safety valves in the Great Depression' *Review of Radical Political Economics* 8, 1, pp.

98-121

Hunter, Monica ((1936) 1961) *Reaction to Conquest* London: Oxford University Press

Irigaray, Luce (1977) 'Women's exile: an interview with Luce Irigaray' *Ideology and Consciousness* 1, pp. 62-76

Jacka, Elizabeth (1977) Contributions to the Theory of Ideology, unpublished PhD thesis, Department of General Philosophy, University of Sydney

Jacka, Marion and Ann Game (1980) The whitegoods industry: the labour process and the sexual division of labour, unpublished paper, School of Behavioural Sciences, Macquarie University, Sydney

James, Selma (1973a) introduction to Dalla Costa *The Power of Women*
— ((1953) 1973b) 'A woman's place' in Dalla Costa *The Power of Women*
— (1972) 1974) *Women, the Unions and Work* Pittsburgh, Pa: Know Inc.

Kahn, A.J. and S.B. Kammerman (eds) (1978) *Family Policy: government and family in fourteen countries* New York: Columbia University Press

Koedt, Anne and Shulamith Firestone (eds) (1971) *Notes from the Third Year: Women's Liberation* New York: Notes from the Second Year Inc.

Komarovsky, Mirra (1964) *Blue-collar Marriage* New York: Random House

Krige, Eileen J. (1964) 'Property, cross-cousin marriage, and the family cycle among the Lobedu' in Gray and Gulliver *The Family Estate in Africa*
— (1974) 'Woman-marriage, with special reference to the Lovedu—its significance for the definition of marriage' *Africa* 44, pp. 11-36

Krige, Eileen J. and J.D. Krige (1943) *The Realm of a Rain-Queen* London: Oxford University Press

Kuhn, Annette (1978) 'Structures of patriarchy and capital in the family' in Kuhn and Wolpe (eds) *Feminism and Materialism*

Kuhn, Annette and Ann-Marie Wolpe (eds) (1978) *Feminism and Materialism: women and the modes of production* London: Routledge and Kegan Paul

Lacan, Jacques (1968a) *The Language of the Self. The Function of Language in Psychoanalysis* transl. with notes and commentary by Anthony Wilden, Baltimore: Johns Hopkins Press
— ((1949) 1968b) 'The mirror-phase as formative of the function of the I' transl. Jean Roussel *New Left Review* 51, pp. 71-77

Lacan, Jacques ((1957) 1972) 'The insistence of the letter in the unconscious' in de George and de George (eds) *The Structuralists*

Laclau, E. (1975) 'The specificity of the political: the Poulantzas-Miliband debate' *Economy and Society* 4, 1, pp. 87-110

Laing, R.D. ((1969) 1972) *The Politics of the Family and Other Essays*

New York: Vintage Books, Random House

Laing, R.D. and A. Esterson ((1964) 1970) *Sanity, Madness and the Family* Harmondsworth, Middlesex: Penguin Books

Lancaster, Jane Beckman (1976) 'Sex roles in primate societies' in Teitelbaum (ed.) *Sex Differences*

Land, H. (1976) 'Women: supporters or supported' in Barker and Allen (eds) *Sexual Divisions and Society*

Land, H. and R. Parker (1978) 'Family policies in Britain: the hidden dimension' in Kahn and Kammerman (eds) *Family Policy*

Lane, Robert (1962) *Political Ideology: Why the American Common Man Believes What He Does* New York: The Free Press

Laslett, Barbara (1974) 'The family as a public and private institution: an historical perspective' in Skolnick and Skolnick (eds) *Intimacy, Family and Society*

Leacock, Eleanor (1958) introduction to 'Social stratification and evolutionary theory: a symposium' *Ethnohistory* 5, 3

— (ed.) (1971) *The Culture of Poverty: A Critique* New York: Simon and Schuster

— (1972) introduction to F. Engels *The Origin of the Family, Private Property and the State* ed. Eleanor Leacock, New York: International Publishers

Lévi-Strauss, Claude (1963) *Structural Anthropology* transl. Claire Jacobson and Brooke G. Schoepf, New York: Basic Books Inc.

— (1969) *The Elementary Structures of Kinship* transl. James H. Bell, John R. von Sturmer and Rodney Needham, London: Eyre and Spottiswoode

Lévi-Strauss, C., M. Augé and M. Godelier (1976) 'Anthropology, history and ideology' *Critique of Anthropology* 2, 6, pp. 44-55

Littlejohn, Gary, Barry Smart, John Wakeford and Nira Yuval-Davis (eds) (1978) *Power and the State* London: Croom Helm

Lockwood, David (1958) *The Blackcoated Worker* London: Unwin University Books

— (1960) 'The "new working class"' *European Journal of Sociology* 1, 2, pp. 248-59

— ((1966) 1975) 'Sources of variation in working class images of society' in Bulmer (ed.) *Working Class Images of Society*

Low, D.A. (1971) *Buganda in Modern History* London: Weidenfeld and Nicolson

Maccoby, Eleanor E. and Carol N. Jacklin (1974) *The Psychology of Sex Differences* California: Stanford University Press

Mackintosh, Maureen (1977) 'Reproduction and patriarchy: a critique of Claude Meillassoux, "Femmes, Greniers et Capitaux"' *Capital and Class* 2, pp. 119-27

Macintyre, Sally (1976) '"Who wants babies?" The social construction of "instincts"' in Barker and Allen (eds) *Sexual Divisions and Society*

Mair, Lucy ((1934) 1965) *An African People in the Twentieth Century* London: Routledge and Kegan Paul

Mainardi, Pat (1970) 'The politics of housework' in Morgan (ed.) *Sisterhood is Powerful*

Makarius, Raoul (1974) 'Structuralism—science or ideology' in Miliband and Saville (eds) *Socialist Register*

Marcuse, Herbert (1972a) *Eros and Civilisation* London: Abacus

— ((1964) 1972b) *One Dimensional Man* London: Abacus

Marx, Karl ((1887) 1971) *Capital* 3 vols, Moscow: Progress Publishers

— ((1857-58) 1973) *Grundrisse. Foundations of the Critique of Political Economy (Rough Draft)* transl. Martin Nicolaus, Harmondsworth, Middlesex: Penguin Books

Marx, Karl and Frederick Engels ((1846) 1969a) *The German Ideology* in Marx and Engels *Selected Works* vol. 1

— ((1848) 1969b) *Manifesto of the Communist Party* in Marx and Engels *Selected Works* vol. 1

— ((1845-95) 1969-70) *Selected Works* 3 vols, Moscow: Progress Publishers

Mathieu, Nicole-Claude (1978) 'Man-culture and woman-nature?' *Women's Studies International Quarterly* 1, 1, pp. 55-65

Matthews, Jill (1984) *Good and Mad Women* Sydney: George Allen and Unwin

Matthiasson, Carolyn J. (ed.) (1974) *Many Sisters: Women in Cross-Cultural Perspective* New York: The Free Press

McDonough, Roisin and Rachel Harrison (1978) 'Patriarchy and relations of production' in Kuhn and Wolpe *Feminism and Materialism*

McIntosh, Mary (1978) 'The state and the oppression of women' in Kuhn and Wolpe *Feminism and Materialism*

McKinlay, John (ed.) (1975) *Processing People: Cases in Organization Behavior* New York: Holt, Rinehart and Winston

McMichael, Tony (ed.) (1972) *Abortion: The Unenforceable Law* Victoria, Australia: Abortion Law Reform Association

McRobbie, Angela (1978) 'Working class girls and the culture of femininity' in Women's Studies Group *Women Take Issue*

Mead, Margaret (ed.) (1937) *Cooperation and Competition Among Primitive Peoples* New York: McGraw-Hill

— (1967) 'The life cycle and its variations: the division of roles' *Daedalus* 96, 3, pp. 871-75

Meillassoux, Claude (1972) 'From reproduction to production' *Economy and Society* 1, 1, pp. 93-105

— (1975) *Femmes, Greniers et Capitaux* Paris: Maspero

— (1981) *Maidens, Meal and Money: Capitalism and the Domestic Community* Cambridge: Cambridge University Press

Miliband, Ralph (1972) 'Reply to Nicos Poulantzas' in Blackburn (ed.) *Ideology in Social Science*

— ((1969) 1973a) *The State in Capitalist Society* London: Quartet Books

— (1973b) 'Poulantzas and the capitalist state' *New Left Review* 82, pp. 83-93

Miliband, Ralph and John Saville (eds) (1974) *Socialist Register* London: Merlin Press

Milkman, Ruth (1976) 'Women's work and economic crisis: some lessons of the Great Depression' *Review of Radical Political Economics* 8, 1, pp. 73-97

Miller, Jay (1974) 'The Delaware as women: a symbolic solution' *American Ethnologist* 1, pp. 507-514

Millett, Kate ((1970) 1972) *Sexual Politics* London: Abacus

Mitchell, Juliet (1971) *Woman's Estate* Harmondsworth, Middlesex: Penguin Books

— (1975) *Psychoanalysis and Feminism* New York: Vintage Books, Random House

Mitchell, Juliet and Ann Oakley (eds) (1976) *The Rights and Wrongs of Women* Harmondsworth, Middlesex: Penguin Books

Mitchell, Juliet and Eli Zaretsky (1974) interview on ABC 'Lateline' program, 3 December

Mohr, James C. (1978) *Abortion in America: The Origins and Evolution of National Policy, 1800-1900* London: Oxford University Press

Molyneux, Maxine (1977) 'Androcentrism in Marxist anthropology' *Critique of Anthropology* 3, 9 and 10, pp. 55-81

Money, John and Anke A. Ehrhardt (1972) *Man and Woman, Boy and Girl* Baltimore: John Hopkins Press

Moore, Barrington Jr. (1969) 'Thoughts on the future of the family' in Edwards (ed.) *The Family and Change*

Morgan, D.H.J. (1975) *Social Theory and the Family* London: Routledge and Kegan Paul

Morgan, Elaine (1972) *The Descent of Woman* London: Souvenir Press

Morgan, Lewis Henry ((1877) 1963) *Ancient Society* ed. with an introduction by Eleanor Leacock, Cleveland, Ohio: Meridian Books

Morgan, Robin (ed.) (1970) *Sisterhood is Powerful* New York: Vintage Books, Random House

Moriarty, Claire (1973) 'Women's rights vs. Catholic dogma: why the church fathers oppose abortion' *International Socialist Review* 34, 3, pp. 8-11, 44-45

Morris, Desmond (1968) *The Naked Ape* London: Corgi Books

Morton, Peggy (1971) 'A woman's work is never done' in Altbach (ed.) *From Feminism to Liberation*

Needham, R. (ed.) (1971) *Rethinking Kinship and Marriage* London: Tavistock Publications

Newson, J. (1963) *Half our Future* report of the Central Advisory Council for Education (England), HMSO

Oakley, Ann (1972) *Sex, Gender and Society* Melbourne: Sun Books
— (1974a) *The Sociology of Housework* London: Martin Robertson
— (1974b) *Housewife* London: Allen Lane, Penguin Books
— (1976) 'Wisewoman and medicine man: changes in the management of childbirth' in Mitchell and Oakley (eds) *The Rights and Wrongs of Women*
O'Brien, Denise (1977) 'Female husbands in Southern Bantu societies' in Schlegel (ed.) *Sexual Stratification*
O'Laughlin, Bridget (1974) 'Mediation of contradiction: why Mbum women do not eat chicken' in Rosaldo and Lamphere (eds) *Woman, Culture and Society*
— (1975) 'Marxist approaches in anthropology' in Siegel (ed.) *Annual Review of Anthropology*
— (1977) 'Production and reproduction: Meillassoux's *Femmes, Greniers et Capitaux' Critique of Anthropology* 2, 8, pp. 3-32
Ortner, Sherry (1974) 'Is female to male as nature is to culture?' in Rosaldo and Lamphere (eds) *Woman, Culture and Society*
Ortner, Sherry (1975) 'Oedipal father, mother's brother, and the penis: a review of Juliet Mitchell's *Psychoanalysis and Feminism' Feminist Studies* 2, 2-3, pp. 167-82
Papers on Patriarchy (1976) papers from the Patriarchy Conference held in London; Lewes, Sussex: Women's Publishing Collective
Pompei, Giuliana (1972) 'Wages for housework', paper distributed by the Cambridge (Mass) Women's Liberation Group, reprinted in *Women: A Journal of Liberation* 3, 3
Poulantzas, Nicos (1972) 'The problem of the capitalist state' in Blackburn (ed.) *Ideology in Social Science*
— (1975) *Political Power and Social Classes,* translation editor Timothy O'Hagan, London: New Left Books
— (1976) 'The capitalist state: a reply to Miliband and Laclau' transl. Rupert Swyer *New Left Review* 95, pp. 63-83
Power, Margaret (1978) Women and economic crises: the Great Depression and the present crisis, paper presented to the Women and Labour Conference, Macquarie University, Sydney, May 1978
Pringle, Rosemary (1980) The sexual division of labour in computing, unpublished paper, School of Behavioural Sciences, Macquarie University, Sydney
Quinn, Naomi (1977) 'Anthropological studies on women's status' in Siegel (ed.) *Annual Review of Anthropology* pp. 181-225
Rathbone, E. (1934) foreword to E. Reiss *Rights and Duties of English Women* London: Sherratt and Hughes
Reed, Evelyn (1969) *Problems of Women's Liberation* New York: Merit Publishers
Reich, Wilhelm ((1946) 1975) *The Mass Psychology of Fascism* Harmondsworth, Middlesex: Penguin Books

Reiche, Reimut ((1968) 1970) *Sexuality and Class Struggle* transl.
    Susan Bennett, London: New Left Books

Reik, Theodor (1948) *Listening with the Third Ear* New York: Grove
    Press Inc.

Reiter, Rayna R. (ed.) (1975) *Toward an Anthropology of Women* New
    York: Monthly Review Press

— (1977) 'The search for origins: unravelling the threads of gender
    hierarchy' *Critique of Anthropology* 3, 9 and 10, pp. 5-24

Rivière, P.G. (1971) 'Marriage: a reassessment' in Needham (ed.)
    Rethinking Kinship and Marriage

Rosaldo, Michelle (1974) 'Woman, culture and society: a theoretical
    overview' in Rosaldo and Lamphere (eds) *Woman, Culture and
    Society*

Rosaldo, Michelle and Louise Lamphere (eds) (1974) *Woman, Culture
    and Society* Stanford, California: Stanford University Press

Roscoe, John (1965) *The Baganda* London: Frank Cass and Co.

Rosenblatt, Jay S. and B. R. Komisaruk (eds) (1977) *Reproductive Beha-
    vior and Evolution* New York: Plenum Press

Rossi, Alice (1977) 'A biosocial perspective on parenting' *Daedalus* 106,
    2, pp. 1-31

Roussel, Jean (1968) 'Introduction to Jacques Lacan' *New Left Review*,
    51, pp. 63-70

Rowbotham, Sheila (1973) *Woman's Consciousness, Man's World*
    Harmondsworth, Middlesex: Penguin Books

Rubery, Jill (1980) 'Structured Labour Markets, Worker Organization
    and Low Pay' in Alice H. Amsden (ed.) *The Economics of Women
    and Work* Harmondsworth, Middlesex: Penguin Books

Rubin, Gayle (1975) 'The traffic in women: notes on the "political
    economy" of sex' in Reiter (ed.) *Toward an Anthropology of Women*

Rubinstein, Linda (1976) 'Do you have a job? An article on wages for
    housework' *Join Hands* (journal of the Communist Party of Austra-
    lia) October, pp. 8-14

Russell, Bertrand ((1929) 1961) *Marriage and Morals* London: Unwin
    Books

Ryan, Penny and Tim Rowse (1975) 'Women, arbitration and the family'
    in Curthoys, Eade and Spearritt (eds) *Women at Work*

Sacks, Karen (1970) 'Social bases for sexual equality: a comparative view'
    in Morgan (ed.) *Sisterhood is Powerful*

— (1971) Economic Bases for Sexual Inequality: A Comparative Study of
    Four African Societies, unpublished PhD thesis, University of
    Michigan

— (1974) 'Engels revisited: women, the organization of production, and
    private property' in Rosaldo and Lamphere (eds) *Woman, Culture
    and Society*

— (1976) 'State bias and women's status' *American Anthropologist* 78, pp. 565-69

Sahlins, Marshall (1968) *Tribesmen* Englewood Cliffs, New Jersey: Prentice-Hall Inc.

— (1974) *Stone Age Economics* London: Tavistock Publications

Schlegel, Alice (ed.) (1977) *Sexual Stratification. A Cross-Cultural View* New York: Columbia University Press

Schneider, David M. and Kathleen Gough (eds) (1961) *Matrilineal Kinship* Berkeley: University of California Press

Seccombe, Wally (1974) 'The housewife and her labour under capitalism' *New Left Review* 83, pp. 3-24

— (1975) 'Domestic labour—reply to critics' *New Left Review* 94, pp. 85-96

— (n.d.) 'The housewife and her labour under capitalism', reprinted with a new postscript in *Red Pamphlet* 8

Seeley, J.R., R.A. Sim and E.W. Loosley (1963) *Crestwood Heights. A Study of the Culture of Suburban Life* New York: John Wiley and Sons Inc.

Sennett, Richard (1970) *Families Against the City* Cambridge, Mass: Harvard University Press

— (1978) interview on ABC 'Broadband' program, 4 April

Sennett, Richard and Jonathan Cobb (1973) *The Hidden Injuries of Class* New York: Vintage Books

Sharp, Rachel and Anthony Green (1975) *Education and Social Control: A Study in Progressive Primary Education* London: Routledge and Kegan Paul

Shorter, Edward (1976) *The Making of the Modern Family* London: Collins

Siegel, Bernard J. (ed.) (1975) *Annual Review of Anthropology* Palo Alto: Annual Review Inc.

— (1977) *Annual Review of Anthropology* Palo Alto: Annual Review Inc.

Singer, Alice (1973) 'Marriage payments and the exchange of people' *Man* 8, 1, pp. 80-92

Skolnick, Arlene and Jerome Skolnick (eds) (1974) *Intimacy, Family and Society* Boston: Little, Brown and Co.

Slater, E. and M. Woodside (1951) *Patterns of Marriage* London: Cassell

Slater, Philip (1970) *The Pursuit of Loneliness* Boston: Beacon Press

Smith, Paul (1978) 'Domestic labour and Marx's theory of value' in Kuhn and Wolpe *Feminism and Materialism*

Stevenson, Mary (1975) 'Women's wages and job segregation' in Edwards et al. *Labor Market Segmentation*

Stoller, Robert J. (1968) *Sex and Gender: On the Development of Masculinity and Femininity* New York: Science House

Strathern, Marilyn (1972) *Women in Between* London: Seminar Press

Szymanski, A. (1976) 'The socialization of women's oppression: a Marxist theory of the changing position of women in advanced capitalist society' *Insurgent Sociologist* 6, 2, pp. 31-58

Teitelbaum, Michael S. (ed.) (1976) *Differences: Social and Biological Perspectives* New York: Anchor Books

Terray, Emmanuel (1972) *Marxism and 'Primitive' Societies* transl. Mary Klopper, New York: Monthly Review Press

Therborn, Göran (1976) 'What does the ruling class do when it rules? Some reflections of different approaches to the study of power in society' *Insurgent Sociologist* 6, 3, pp. 3-16

— (1978) *What does the Ruling Class do when it Rules?* London: New Left Books

Thom, Martin (1976) 'The unconscious structured like a language' *Economy and Society* 5, 4, pp. 435-69

Tiffany, Sharon W. (1978) 'Models and the social anthropology of women: a preliminary assessment' *Man* 13, 1, pp. 34-51

Tiger, Lionel (1969) *Men in Groups* New York: Random House

Tiger, Lionel and Robin Fox (1971) *The Imperial Animal* New York: Holt, Rinehart and Winston

Tiger, Lionel and Joseph Shepher ((1975) 1977) *Women in the Kibbutz* Harmondsworth, Middlesex: Penguin Books

Timpanaro, Sebastiano (1974) 'Considerations on materialism' *New Left Review* 85, pp. 3-22

— (1975) *On Materialism* London: New Left Books

Torsh, Daniela (ed.) (1976) *A Women's Education Catalogue* Carlton, Victoria: Greenhouse Publications

Turnbull, Colin ((1972) 1974) *The Mountain People* London: Picador, Pan Books

Veltmeyer, H. (1974-75) 'Towards an assessment of the structuralist interrogation of Marx, Claude Lévi-Strauss and Louis Althusser' *Science and Society* 38, 4, pp. 385-421

Vogel, Lise (1973) 'The earthly family' *Radical America* 7, 4-5, pp. 9-44

Vort-Ronald, Pat (1974) 'Women and class' *Refractory Girl* 7, pp. 20-26

Warrior, Betsy (1971) 'Slavery, or labor of love?' in Koedt and Firestone (eds) *Notes from the Third Year: Women's Liberation*

Warrior, Betsy and Lisa Leghorn (1974) *Houseworker's Handbook* c/o Women's Center, 46 Pleasant Street, Cambridge, Mass

Westergaard, J.H. (1972) 'Sociology: the myth of classlessness' in Blackburn (ed.) *Ideology in Social Science*

West, Jackie (ed.) (1982) *Work, Women and the Labour Market* London: Routledge and Kegan Paul

Willis, Paul (1977) *Learning to Labour. How working class kids get working class jobs* Farnborough, Hants, England: Saxon House

Wilson, Elizabeth (1974) 'Women and the welfare state' *Red Rag Pamphlet* no. 2, London: Red Rag Collective

— (1977) *Women and the Welfare State* London: Tavistock Publications

Wollheim, R. (1975) 'Psychoanalysis and feminism' *New Left Review* 93, pp. 61-69

Women and Labour Conference Papers (1978) papers of the Conference held at Macquarie University, Sydney, May 1978; published by the Convenors, School of History, Philosophy and Politics, Macquarie University

Women's Bureau, Department of Labour (1974) *O.E.C.D. Study. The Role of Women in the Economy, (Women and Work* No. 12), Women's Bureau, Department of Labour, Canberra: AGPS

Women's Research and Resources Centre (1977) *The Main Enemy: a materialist analysis of women's oppression* London

Women's Studies Group (1978) *Women Take Issue* Centre for Contemporary Cultural Studies, University of Birmingham, London: Hutchinson

Working Papers in Sex, Science and Culture (1976) 1, Nos. 1 and 2, Sydney University

Young, M.F.D. (ed.) (1971) *Knowledge and Control: New Directions for the Sociology of Education* London: Collier-Macmillan

Young, Michael and Peter Willmott (1957) *Family and Kinship in East London* London: Routledge and Kegan Paul

Zaretsky, Eli (1975) 'Male supremacy and the unconscious' *Socialist Revolution* 21-22, pp. 7-55

— ((1973) 1976) *Capitalism, The Family and Personal Life* London: Pluto Press

Index

subordination work, family and,
33-56, 118, 127; paid and
unpaid, xvi, 43-4, 57-85,
118-19, 126, 128, 130-32;
personal fulfilment and, 46, 65;
white collar, 51-3; 135n5;
women's, 18, 29; women's,
devaluation of, 126; women's,
paid, 50, 53-4, 64, 72-3, 75,
83-6, 107, 111, 130, 132,
138n15; *see also* domestic
labour; exploitation; housewives;
labour market; manual/mental
labour; productive labour; sexual
division of labour; unproductive
labour; wage labour; women;
working class
work incentive, 108, 110
working class, the, xiii, xviii,
44-6, 48, 50-51, 68, 72-4, 77,
79-81, 83-5, 115, 121, 124,
129, 131, 136n9, 137n14;
family, 17, 45, 51, 54, 71-2, 81,
124-5; schools, 121, 123,
125-6; *see also* class; men,
working class; privatised
worker; wage labour; women,
working class; work
working-class movement, *see*
trade unions
working-class strategies, 46-7, 52,
80, 84-5, 120-22, 124, 126,
128-9, 133
World War II, 75, 106, 112

Young, M.F., 139n5
Young, M., and Willmott, P.,
134n6

Zaretsky, E., 41-7, 55, 77, 88, 96